The Priest Who Left His Religion

The Priest Who Left His Religion

IN PURSUIT OF COSMIC SPIRITUALITY

JOHN SHIELDS

FOREWORD AND AFTERWORD BY BRIONY PENN, PH.D.

INTRODUCTION BY NIKKI IYOLO SANCHEZ

Monkfish Book Publishing Company
Rhinebeck, New York

Paperback ISBN 978-1-948626-35-4
eBook ISBN 978-1-948626-36-1

Library of Congress Cataloging-in-Publication Data

Names: Shields, John, 1938-2017, author. | Penn, Briony, 1960- writer of
    supplementary textual content. | Sanchez, Nikki, 1986- writer of
    introduction.
Title: The priest who left his religion : in pursuit of cosmic spirituality
    / John Shields ; foreword and afterword by Briony Penn, Ph.D.
Description: [Second edition]. | Rhinebeck, New York : Monkfish Book
    Publishing Company, [2020]
Identifiers: LCCN 2020041395 (print) | LCCN 2020041396 (ebook) | ISBN
    9781948626354 (paperback) | ISBN 9781948626361 (ebook)
Subjects: LCSH: Shields, John, 1938-2017. | Catholic ex-priests--United
    States--Biography. | Catholic ex-priests--British Columbia--Biography.
Classification: LCC BX4668.3.S54 A3 2020 (print) | LCC BX4668.3.S54
    (ebook) | DDC 282.092 [B]--dc23
LC record available at https://lccn.loc.gov/2020041395
LC ebook record available at https://lccn.loc.gov/2020041396

Monkfish Book Publishing Company
22 East Market Street, Suite 304
Rhinebeck, NY 12572
(845) 876-4861
monkfishpublishing.com

Contents

Foreword

By Briony Penn, Ph.D., a Canadian geographer, author, artist, and land rights activist who received international attention when she protested logging on Salt Spring Island by riding horseback through downtown Vancouver (un)dressed as Lady Godiva

When I was growing up in Victoria, on the West Coast of Canada, you couldn't help but hear about John Shields. He was frequently in the news then as the head of the biggest union in British Columbia, negotiating equitable salaries for women, advocating nondiscriminatory hiring, or in the midst of some other battle for social justice. He was often on the TV at night, his pulpit voice projecting a blend of toughness and compassion. He never seemed to stumble, lose his temper, or falter in his conviction of what was fair. This was never more evident than when he challenged one of his own—the union boss of the woodworkers' union—after taking a trip into the decimated ancient forests, where he felt the union had gone too far in its exploitation of the natural world. It was an act of spirit, one that was characteristic of this former priest's journey to stand up against dogma and find spirituality in all of the cosmos.

John was universally admired, even by those who didn't stand to gain by his tenaciousness. For a young woman like me, his authority and skills of negotiating for equity in a world of inequity, power, and influence were aspired to but seemed impossibly unattainable—as if from another galaxy. I'd started on my own little battles to defend small things like wildflowers, oak trees, lizards, and streams, but I had no inkling that our worlds would one day fuse and that there would be a commonality in our beliefs and ideas.

Twenty years later, John met my best friend, Robin June Hood, who became his second wife, and I was welcomed into their orbit. John shared his many stories, the content of which you will read in this book—a fusing of personal memoir charting his philosophical evolution from priest to social rights counselor and activist to cosmologist and nurturer of spirit and earth, with parallel public discourse over the last sixty years of developments in the fields of quantum physics, ecology, astronomy, anthropology, and theology.

Many people encouraged John to write this book because he was uniquely positioned to bring the worlds of spirit and science together in an accessible form. He had access to the theological colleges, laboratories, astronomical observatories, union bargaining table, parliaments, long houses, and counseling clinics where these ideas were formed. He synthesized those experiences and theories and brought them to us in a way that we can all relate to both publicly and privately—in a personal memoir with interpretations and applications formed by a life devoted to service.

Many people ask: How do you marry spirit with science? How do you find spiritual meaning in the secular age or hang onto the wonder of science in the face of many religions' increasingly orthodox dogma? And how do you take such ideas and offer them to someone who is dying or has a hungry child or is struggling with grief or difficult issues of governance to help them get through the day?

Cosmology offers an elegant solution to these questions, and this book provides a priest's journey to that answer from his first orthodox training in the Catholic church in his native New York City to his awakening with the civil rights movement, Martin Luther King, and the radical theologians to his encounters with the First Nations' traditional ecological wisdom and coastal British Columbia's ancient forest. John demonstrated that we are at a profound point in human history: We have the ability to know more than we have ever known about the minutiae of scientific discovery and at the same time, embrace a spiritual tradition that bridges the ancient with the modern.

Reading this book reminds me of the way it felt to be at the dinner table with John. At John's table, everyone felt included and present in the grand unfolding of evolution. The twin stories of the cosmos and his life bind us all together with an equalizing force. No matter whom he wrote about, from his compromised steelworker father who found it difficult to express his parental love, to his first wife with her mystical struggles, the eyes of those portrayed catch the same sparkle of light released at the conception of the universe. In John's universe, everyone, from the trees that offered him solace during his first seminary retreats, to the young woman he came to adopt full heartedly in his second marriage, was made from the same stardust and fueled by the same solar energy. This book is a celebration of the knowledge that all of our emerging consciousnesses came from the same origins and together we are all creating a future.

Many readers will enjoy being in the company of someone who has explored the paradoxes of religion and spirituality. Here is a man who was at birth predicted to be the first North American pope, but then shed all of his early promise and training to question orthodoxy. Like John, I come from a long tradition of theologians and missionaries (one of my ancestors was named Christian Church), so I have some experience in the virtues and disasters of orthodox faiths. My grandfather was an Anglican missionary in India and then returned to England to be a vicar of a country parish. I only knew my grandfather back in England, where he conducted services of great beauty, especially around harvest time when all of the local parishioners would bring their produce to be blessed in the old Norman church. My grandmother, who was my deepest influence, had a grounded simple faith based on kindness to all beings—human and animal. When I visited, we walked the woodlands and meadows around her small cottage, greeting the bluebells, parishioners, and badgers alike. This shaped my understanding of Christianity, but I couldn't reconcile this institution with the same church that abducted children of First Nations from their homes and placed them in residential schools. I believe many readers will recognize themselves in John's recounting of the crisis of faith he experienced when the Catholic Church abandoned the principles of equity and speaking truth to power that moment of faltering faith, along with his long, difficult journey to find something to replace it. John put up signposts for replenishing the cup that anyone from a lapsed orthodox faith will appreciate. In my own experience of reading this book, I ended up back where I started as a child—walking like my grandmother in nature.

In this regard, John's story is as vitally important for women as it is for men, though for different reasons. Like my grandmother, I shine when I am outdoors, sharing the joy, paradoxes, and humor of my home-place, with all its warts and wonder. I have tried to venture into positions of power in order to protect those intangible qualities—the glint of a lizard's eye, the sweet taste of fresh water, the coolness and light of an ancient forest, a safe wildflower meadow where my boys tumbled in the sun—but the warrior's armour didn't fit. John always represented to me someone who could carry the sword well. But a key part of his book is his insight into perpetuating only those archetypes. It is tempting for those of us who don't see ourselves as White Knights or Lone Rangers to undervalue our contributions, or worse, to long for someone to save us. John's years of self-reflection and personal work explore the archetypes that powerful men carry, and his own failures to live up to them. According to John, behaving like the Lone Ranger or believing that the Lone Ranger will solve our problems inhibits our ability to address the big issues, both environmental and social, that are facing us. Warrior archetypes that may once have served us well once, in a different time and place, are not serving us well in the twenty-first century. John's voice is like the last bark of the silverback primate urging the troop to drop his lone authority and adopt a more collective form of governance and spirituality. It is the last order but the most important one, and, ironically, it would take someone of his authority to issue it. This book is a call to both men and women alike to assume new roles.

For anyone interested in the curious and frightening turn that society has recently taken—disintegrating democracies; the growing manipulation of the many by the few through fear, ideology, and rhetoric—this book also offers a very personal insight into a similar time, the 1960s, when Pope John XXIII's reforms were turned back by his successor. We need powerful stories for our time that remind us of the constant vigilance needed, the advances that were once made and the shift towards commonality that is required to achieve them. The cosmological story does that. It is as easily adopted by someone who is deeply committed to science as it is by someone who is bound to religion. It offers common ground.

Which leads to the final gift of this book: the celebration of what an expanding worldview, celebrating all creation, brings to our lives at both a personal and a global level. Living with an expanded worldview makes you happier, wanting for less, and, therefore, you can live easier on this fragile Earth of ours. We latch onto personal stories because they are what interest us most and they're what we can most easily comprehend. But John's story also demonstrates that a cosmological worldview could shape a very different collective future. After leaving the priesthood, John used the scientific revelations of the time to forge a life of discovery, joy, spirituality, and inclusion of even the smallest creatures—and his story is vital for our time.

Introduction

By Nikki Iyolo Sanchez, a Pipil/Maya and Irish/Scottish academic, Indigenous media-maker, decolonial and environmental educator, and community organizer, and John Shields's stepdaughter

As far back as I can remember, I said a singular prayer every night before I fell asleep: "Dear God, please bring my mom someone who loves her as much as I do." When I was sixteen, my mother suffered a heart episode and almost died. At the time, I was working at a trendy restaurant in downtown Victoria, Canada, and I will never forget my manager calling me into the kitchen to take the call. I stood there, paralyzed, until my manager told me to go to the hospital. During that ten minute drive, I realized, viscerally, that my mother was the only true family I had in this world. She survived the episode, but during her recovery we had to give up so much, including our home. I stopped praying, and my faith was replaced by a deep sense of injustice and anger.

With a sense of urgency, I moved to Montreal to pursue a bachelor of arts degree at McGill University with the singular focus of establishing myself in a career so that my mother would always be taken care of—I no longer wanted to rely on prayer. About six months into my first year at McGill, my mom became uncharacteristically brief during our phone calls and was unusually flighty when I asked her what was going on. It wasn't until my return home to Canada's West Coast the following summer that I discovered that she had fallen in love.

When I first met John Shields, it was a sunny day. All my mother had told me about him was that he was a magical man who spoke to animals. John was wearing a paperboy hat and offered to drop me off at my next engagement in his burnt-red, two-seater Miata.

John and I met at what was most likely my least graceful stage in life. I was emerging from a lifetime of trauma, abuse, and neglect, and my teenage turbulence was coming to a crescendo. Any suitor of my mother's in his right mind would have taken one look at me and run for the hills, but not John. He was patient and kind, and stern only when necessary.

To paint a picture of who we were when we found one another, John was a writer whose singular gift to himself was his Miata, and who was looking forward to a peaceful golden age, while I was an angsty and defiant nineteen-year-old with little capacity to accommodate anyone who stepped in my path. But somehow, our meeting was one of the universe's delightful, mysterious gifts, and we fit perfectly. We bonded within a few months over our shared love of cooking and animals. I wanted a dog, and in a final attempt to win my approval, John conceded, after months of my aggressive campaign, to adopt a puppy together one weekend while my mom was away. Diego, our Cairn terrier, and Italian cooking became the glue that held our family together. For the first time in my entire life, family dinners became a norm and I had someone listed in my cell phone contacts "in case of emergency" who would actually pick up the phone. In the years that followed, John and I came to know and love each other most deeply through our conversations, which began after family dinners and continued late into the night, about the nature of the universe and how to best harness our lives to enact goodness and love on Earth.

When John decided to write this book, I was deeply concerned. I was acutely cognizant of the slow rate of his typing and worried that it would take him decades. But, true to form, once he committed to a vision, he saw it through. During the years he was writing this book, I remember passing by the open room of his office and hearing the slow but consistent clacks of his keyboard and his melodious voice, as he often sang songs by Eva Cassidy or Joni Mitchell while he worked.

From the first time I met John, there was something magical about him that I am still struggling to put into words. He was truly a man of his time and culture—an Irish American, born in 1938 in New York City, who loved watching American football and ate grits religiously on Sundays—but he also profoundly expanded his consciousness and compassion until the day he died. I'll never forget his kindnesses. Once, while I was working at a remote wilderness resort in Clayoquot Sound, British Columbia, my mentor and Elder, Qaamina Sam, informed me that he had been called to testify for the Truth and Reconciliation Commission. He asked for my support, but I was unable to get out of work so I called John and requested that he go in my place. Without question, he and my mother drove five hours to stand in solidarity as my Elder shared each instance of violence, abuse and trauma he endured during the decade he was held in residential school. Despite never having met before that day, John forged a deep connection with Qaamina. From then on, John devoted himself to seeking both my own and Qaamina's counsel regarding how he could direct his influence towards repatriation, decolonization, and reconciliation.

Slow, steady, and ever consistent, John seemed like someone who would live forever. His presence in my life gave me a gift greater than I could ever have conceived to ask for. His love for and commitment to me and my mother allowed me to forge my own way forward. I no longer had to act out of scarcity, urgency, or deficit. Knowing that my mother was loved and cared for, and certain that my "in case of emergency" person would pick up the phone, I felt for the first time that I had permission to follow my own path. Despite my having abandoned prayer, and even my faith, my childhood prayer had been answered.

But in 2015, shortly after the first edition of this book was published in Canada, John and my mother had a car crash, and in the aftermath, John was diagnosed with a rare condition called amyloidosis. There are two types of this disease, one curable and the other terminal. I was living in Toronto then, but had gone home to British Columbia to help out after John and my mother were released from the hospital following the accident. There happened to be a federal election taking place. In addition to our love of food, philosophy, and dogs, John and I also loved talking about politics. While waiting in a very long line for advanced voting, I sent John a text saying, "This is brutal." He must not have received the preceding message, telling him that I was waiting to vote, because his response came in a lengthy email message. That was a miscommunication for which I will forever be grateful, for the email so perfectly encapsulates the brilliance and grace of the man I am so privileged to call my father.

Dear Nikki,

When I read "brutal" last night, I was surmising that you had read the information on the Mayo Clinic website. I am also assuming that it was hard for you to assimilate. Since I have been thinking about it a lot, I wanted to share some of my thoughts with you.

The Christian worldview supposes that an all-powerful creator is the direct cause of everything that happens in this world. That is why people pray to God to receive a different outcome when faced with unwelcome news. I have long ago rejected that notion. I don't believe that any divine being wills pain or misfortune on creatures. Such a being would be a monster with a sadistic streak. Ever since I discovered the scientific findings that evolving energy is responsible for the development of the universe and everything in it, I have dispensed with the idea of a creator. [It is] a more primitive explanation for the world that is now redundant.

Perhaps I have a legacy of religious thinking, but I don't think so. I have concluded that the cosmos is sentient, conscious in ways that we have yet to discover. I believe that we, and everything in the universe, reflect the source. We are part of an evolving flow of living development, deriving our form from the evolutionary creatures from which we descend. Our brains, with its ascending development from reptile to mammalian predecessors are a perfect indicator of what I mean. We use our brains, increasing consciousness, perfecting the flow of evolution if we live up to our potential. We are integral to continuing evolution, affecting the entire cosmos. Like us, the universe is tending to the benign and the good.

We are like holons, simultaneously a whole and a part. Like nesting Russian dolls, we are made up of a near infinity of smaller holons, like particles, atoms, molecules, cells, organs, etc., and we are nested in a near infinity of larger holons—family, community, ecologies, galaxies, etc. Everything smaller and larger affects us. And in turn, we affect everything else up to and including the universe.

When I reflect on the fact that I have amyloids in my blood, I think of it as analogous to cancer. A defective protein is a remnant of our evolutionary past. It is also a holon. Something in its survival history gave it an advantage by folding to keep from being assimilated by the other cells in the body. Nothing could be more natural. It is the effect on my body as a whole organism that shows up the evolutionary lag.

My hope is that the type of amyloidosis I have is the kind that will respond to the known treatments. But whichever type, it is what it is and I can live with that. There is no intervention that can change what is. Some may consider that fatalistic, but I don't see it that way. I have lived fully and effectively. I may have more that I will be able to accomplish in whatever time I am given.

Whether my lifespan is shorter or longer, I want to continue to be in the present moment. I am conscious that I am loved, and that I have added good to the environment that supports me.

While my mind sees all this clearly, my heart is deeply affected by my love of you and Robin. I love you as you with the whole gamut of virtues and faults. You are more than your mother's daughter. To me, you are a ray of light that has come into my life and welcomed me into yours. You are my daughter, and there is nothing that needs to be added to that.

Do not let your sadness and grief dominate your other consciousness. We need to be able to be authentic and to know that in the present moment there is joy and happiness to be had. Don't allow yourself to be pulled away from that with longings to be elsewhere. We each will walk the path before us. Know that I am okay. What is, is. And at bedrock, I love you.

As a whitewater kayaker, you know that you need to be conscious of the dynamics in order to be able to respond instinctively to what they demand. So it is in life. Stay focused and alert and the rest will unfold as it will.

With all my heart,

John

My father had a knack for the infinite and the eternal. As it would be, in his usual unconventional and entirely serendipitous way, he was sought out by the *New York Times* during the last months of his life to share his story of choosing an assisted death. Of course, he said yes. My mother and I were both too distraught to protest and fully aware that debating this decision with John would be futile. So, as strange as the rest of the experience was, we also had a team present from one of the world's biggest newspapers as we held hands, white-knuckled, and marched with John towards his final breath.

John's last weeks with us were surreal, but I remember that his eyes became clearer and clearer and were always just as sparkly as ever. To his very last day, he continued to surprise and delight us. I slept under his hospice bed the night before we had to say goodbye and somehow found the courage to sit by his side as he took his last breaths. While the doctor was preparing his doses, and our dog Diego sat by his side, John sang with a childlike smile on his face, "Who could ask for anything more?" I held his hand in mine long after his heart had stopped beating, and he never loosened his grip.

Two months later, during the lunch break at a conference I was attending, an email came through. The *New York Times* article about John had been published, and it was on the front cover. I sat down alone and wept while I read the account of his last days. It was as though he had reached through time and come back to give me one last kiss. Suddenly, I understood why he had consented to the intrusive process of documenting his final days. He truly did have a knack for understanding how to exist as eternal.

It wasn't until after John's death that my mother and I fully came to understand the impact he'd had on the world—the depth of his commitment to justice, equity, and truth, and the extent of his sacrifice. While he was alive, it was not uncommon for a former nurse to see him in the grocery store and stop to profess what his campaign for wage equity had meant for her family, or for a former foster child to bump into us on the street and share a story about how John's kindness had forever marked his or her life. But following John's death came an outpouring of stories of his heroism, his kindness, and his childlike humor. It left my mother and I stunned, and smiling.

I would be lying if I said we didn't miss John greatly, but in moments of profound beauty and grace I can still feel his eyes sparkling beside me. This book is a gift to us all, and in its pages he lives on. As someone who knew John by heart, I can tell you that he generously shared his knowledge and his love. He never wanted to replace someone else's ideas with his own; rather, he sought dialogue and reciprocal exchange.

If I could offer one instruction for reading the pages ahead, it would be to approach John's words as an invitation for rich consideration and evolving discourse. My memories of my father will always be of the sparkle in his eyes dancing with the flickering candlelight at our dinner table as he shared with deep humility his perspectives and cumulative wisdom about the nature of the universe and human life on Earth. As you journey through his pages, I invite you to create your own memories of him, because his love, like his legacy, is truly eternal, and the wisdom he left behind is meant just as much for you as it is for me.

The First American Pope

Tell me, what is it you plan to do
With your one wild and precious life?
—Mary Oliver

W HEN I WAS a baby, my grandfather held me in his out-
stretched arms and proclaimed that I would be the first
American Pope.

On May 8, 1965, I was ordained a Roman Catholic priest. The
sanctuary of my order's mother church was rich with the smell
of incense and the echoes of the choir, and a sense of the sacred
embraced everyone who was there. As I walked from the altar,
where the Cardinal had just anointed my hands, to the communion
rail, where my family awaited my first blessing, I was overcome by
the significance of that day. It was the culmination of a prophecy.
Next to my mother and father, my beloved grandmother beamed.
She remembered what her husband had foretold about me. She
held a dream in her heart.

I had left home at the age of seventeen and spent the next ten
years being educated for the priesthood, and then joining the

Paulist Fathers. I was the only son of devout Irish-Catholic parents, and my ordination was the fulfillment of a family dream. For me, it was also the culmination of sacrifice and hard work, as well as deep and wrenching change.

Just as I began my studies in the major seminary, Pope John XXIII convened the Second Vatican Council, an ecumenical council through which he intended to renew Roman Catholicism. By coincidence, my teachers were priests who had been close to the preparation for the Council and had studied with the theologians who would write the Council documents for the bishops. Vatican II turned out to be the most far-reaching renewal event that the Catholic Church could remember, and it would indelibly change my life.

My priesthood would be defined by my assignment to teach the theology that emerged from the renewal mandate, and by a pope who would destroy my faith by denying the Council's implications.

There was no Garden of Eden

The Vatican Council changed every aspect of my preparation for the priesthood, as it worked on reforms intended to update and renew the way the Church thought about itself and acted in the modern world. My teachers used the text that their teachers were producing in Rome, which gave me the opportunity to learn almost firsthand the basis for the Church's renewal. Among the most significant parts of the document was the one on Sacred Scripture. The Council bishops debated and then voted on a mandate for change. Scholars who understood the thinking behind the Council documents shared their insights in class.

All of the documents enacted by the Council were intended to impact the way the Church would express itself in the future. What I learned in seminary radically changed my understanding of Catholic teaching. Over the course of six years, I had to relinquish beliefs that I had learned as a student in religion classes. In graduate theology school, studying the Scriptures, I found profound changes in the way the modern Church thought about the Bible. Starting in the mid-twentieth century, Protestant, Catholic, and Jewish biblical experts around the world had been discovering new information about the Scriptures. The agreement among the experts about the new information required entirely new interpretation of the sacred texts.

As I was exposed to the new insights, I often felt lightheaded, as if I were breathing rarified air. Many of the discoveries made in seminary shook my faith in the Church's infallibility to its foundation. As I studied the Book of Genesis, one of the most important books of the Old Testament, I realized how much modern scholars had changed what most Roman Catholics commonly understood.

Scholars had discovered that Genesis was not as old as everyone once thought, and that Moses could not have written it. I had learned in church school that Genesis is one of the five books of Moses, but it was created five hundred to a thousand years after the time that Moses was thought to have lived, and a mere five hundred years before the time of Christ. The scholars agreed that it was not history.

And there was no actual Garden of Eden. Scriptural exports

agreed that the authors of Genesis—whoever they were—were not asserting that there was an actual couple called Adam and Eve. There was no snake, no fall of man, and no Original Sin. Instead, these were simply characters in a mythic story designed to teach theology, not an actual history of the origin of the world.

I was shocked and disturbed when I first learned these findings. Centuries of fighting between the Church and science could have been avoided if this knowledge had been available earlier.

What the Church had taught in the past was mistaken

When the Vatican Council adopted the findings of the best biblical scholars, the assembly of the world's bishops made a bold break with the past. They asserted that, in order to interpret the Bible, a reader must understand the literary style and the intention of the author of the book. Consequently, what the Church had taught in the past was mistaken, and there was an urgent need to correct the ramifications of that error.

The evidence that was becoming available was strong and irrefutable. I examined the evidence from history, from internal critical analysis of the texts, and from external historical evidence such as the conquest of Babylon by the Persians, and was completely won over to the new conclusions. That enabled me to relinquish my earlier held beliefs, which were based on incomplete knowledge.

By embracing the new discoveries about Genesis, the Council opened the door to a significant reinterpretation of some of the

Church's key teachings. If there was no Adam or Eve, and there was no Garden of Eden, then there was no Original Sin.

The Council did not deal with the implications of this new understanding of the Bible. This was left to theologians to accomplish after the council was over. I was aghast when Paul VI, who succeeded John XXIII in 1963, rejected the key teaching of the bishops at the Council. In his proclamation, Pope Paul admitted that the truth would be too upsetting to church members.

A new explanation of the Christian religion

With no fall from grace, humanity did not need to be redeemed. The Gospels taught that Jesus's message was a message of love. It made sense for the Church to reexamine Christ's mission to emphasize the shift from law to love. He could be seen as an example of God's love rather than as a human sacrifice who died for our sins. The anticipation of participating in a new explanation of the Christian religion exhilarated me as I set out on my first assignment as a priest.

I discovered that very few teachers had been trained in the new theology. Only a handful of bishops placed an emphasis on teaching of the Vatican II philosophy. The retrenchment to the pre-Council positions came so quickly that the new teaching never made it into seminary curricula for priestly training.

As a result, very few clergy were prepared for the sweeping changes that the Council had introduced, and their resistance to change was high. Most of them even resisted turning the altar to face the people, and praying the Mass in English.

My role as a new priest had been to teach the new Vatican Council theology. The Council was still in session when I began my first assignment. As a teacher, I found the people avidly welcomed the message of the Council and were ready to adopt its thinking. The clergy, however, were fearful of the changes that the Council required. They rejected the message—and the messenger. I was transferred from my post after two years. By then Pope Paul was rejecting the teaching of the Council.

The Pope wanted to silence all the eminent theologians who would bear witness to the truth

The Vatican Curia reacted swiftly to cover up all of the evidence of the Council's teaching about the Bible. The experts who advised the bishops were systematically removed from their teaching positions in Catholic universities. It was as if the pope wanted to silence all of the eminent theologians who would bear witness to the truth he was rejecting.

After only four years as a priest, although my position as religious education director at the parish at the University of Texas was relatively minor, my superior silenced me because of the effect my teaching was having. He removed me from my role as director of education and actually prohibited me from preaching in the parish. My role was over. The Church had changed direction and it was time for me to leave.

I was devastated. The impact set me reeling. Without a parish or a classroom, my role as a priest had ended. The force of the experience led me to leave the clergy and the Church. This crisis started me on my journey from religion to spirituality.

o o o

Up until that point, religion had been my whole life. I'd had a relationship with God since I was a young boy. I had a picture of the Sacred Heart of Jesus in my bedroom at my parents' home in New York City. My mother went to Mass regularly—not only on Sundays, but on the nine first Fridays of the year as well. Although my father was not so devout, he considered himself religious. My parents' friends were all Catholic, and they counted priests among them, from their own pre-married days. I can't remember when I first wanted to be a priest, but I know that by high school I was conscious of a quiet longing. Some people say there are no accidents, but at the time, my entry into Brooklyn Prep felt like a happenstance.

I went to the Catholic elementary school in our parish. My family wanted me to receive a solid education in my faith. In reality, the parochial school education was less than ideal. Sixty children sat in desks that were bolted to the floor in rows six across and ten deep. I got very little personal attention. No teacher spotted my dyslexia. Because of the demand for admissions, the school had two entry periods, September and January. I was in the January group.

When I was ready for high school, my mother learned of a school in Brooklyn run by the Jesuits that offered an accelerated program, enabling students to finish high school early, in three and a half years. I passed the admission tests. The down side was that I would need to commute, by bus and subway, for an hour and a half, each way. Despite the obstacles, I enrolled in Brooklyn Prep's accelerated program.

I quickly learned to respect and admire the Jesuits who taught me. As teachers, and as men, they were exemplary. They were tough if they needed to be, and solicitous in their care for their students. For the first time, I had brilliant teachers who took an interest in me and loved what they taught. In my first year, I had a history teacher who made American history come alive. I found myself excelling in academic work as well. I played on the football team and was considered for a future football scholarship to college.

Then at the start of my second year, there was an unfortunate incident that changed some things at Brooklyn Prep for me. During a football game, I broke my nose. I thought it a badge of honor in a tough sport, but my mother was horrified. Any disfiguring of my face was abhorrent to her. She made me promise to give up football altogether. I felt shame for obeying her. One of the Jesuits, the dean of discipline, belittled me for being a sissy. I blamed myself for giving in to my mother's fear. My reaction to the incident affected my feeling of belonging, and before the end of the end of the year my grades slumped. I did not see the connection at the time, nor could I talk to my mother about it.

But in other ways, I was blossoming. My English teacher that year was Father Daniel Berrigan. He would later become the leading Catholic critic of the war in Viet Nam. He repeatedly protested the draft, and served a three-year prison sentence for his courageous actions. He founded Plough Shares, a leading nonviolent organization, to promote peace and to end the Viet Nam War.

When I met Father Berrigan, he was a young priest, slightly built and surprisingly shy. His angular features and intense manner projected self-respect. I admired him from our first meeting. He invited some of the boys from my class to become involved in social action, and told us about some people who were not getting a fair deal from their neighborhood. He suggested that we could make a difference in the lives of our neighbors. I enrolled in his program called the Sodality, based on the principles of the *see, judge, act*, method of approaching and assessing situations.

My involvement with the Sodality seemed like an honor to my family. My parents were thrilled that I was developing a relationship with the priests and fascinated by the organization I was joining.

Father Berrigan took us to a Bedford-Stuyvesant, Brooklyn, housing project that was experiencing what looked like vandalism, and assigned us to observe the situation and come back with solutions. We discovered that the new residents were scavenging wood from banisters and windowsills to use as wood for cook stoves. It was not vandalism, but an absence of life skills, which could be easily resolved. I learned by working with Father Berrigan and the others that I could make the world more just. I was able to watch a priest, who was my teacher, directly influence the world for the better. I wanted to have that influence on the world, too.

At the end of third year, I decided to try the seminary. I chose the Paulists because of their excellent reputation in New York City for preaching and their work on the radio. I would be going from Brooklyn Prep to the minor seminary of St. Peter's College in

Catonsville, Maryland, on the outskirts of Baltimore, to find out if I could be a priest. My mother was overjoyed that I was taking that step, although she was upset that I would be leaving home and living so far away. I could not tell her that I wanted distance from her tight emotional control. My dad had difficulty expressing what he felt, but he let me know that he wasn't sure that a life of celibacy was something he wanted for me; nonetheless, he supported my going.

I was excited by the prospect of studying to become a priest. Regardless of the legend of my grandfather's prediction that I would be the first American pope, the ideal work that was close to God continually beckoned to me. As a teen, I had felt romantic about the priesthood. Looking back through the lens of my later experience, I realize that I also saw the possibility of living a holy life as the fulfillment of my idea of the Church.

For the next three years, my classes were small, with only about seven to fifteen men in each one. I learned Greek and Latin, and I followed a Classics course in preparation for entering the major seminary to study philosophy and theology. The simplicity of the seminary routine suited my contemplative nature. My world slowed down. We followed the Church's liturgical cycle from season to season. The rituals of the liturgy stirred me deeply. I saw them as a portal to a deeper mysticism that transported me into a timeless state. Even singing in the ancient Latin added to the mystique.

My favorite season was Easter. The Church's reenactment of the death and resurrection mysteries made a profound impression on me. For the first time, I kept vigil on Holy Thursday, kneeling before the altar for hours at a time, a practice I would repeat every year for the next ten years of my studies. I felt an intense closeness to Jesus Christ, the Prince of Peace, and thought of myself as following in his footsteps.

Prayer became direct communication. Alone in the plain, wood-paneled chapel, my imagination allowed me to develop a personal sense of connection with Christ. The Savior became my intimate companion, and I spent many hours in conversation with him. Kneeling in the early morning darkness, I had a strong sense of his presence.

The first few years in the seminary convinced me that I wanted to become a priest, and I was prepared for the demands that life as a priest required. The biggest concern I had was about the requirement for celibacy. Although I had never had sex, I was not sure I could live without intimacy or physical love and joy. That seemed like an endless sacrifice that might be beyond my capabilities.

Seminarians at the early stages of their education were allowed to go home for the summer, so I decided that my visit home would be a time to test my inner resolve. I felt I had to determine whether I could leave the seminary to live among my friends and still pursue the ideal of celibacy each summer.

My parents had a cottage on Peconic Bay in Southampton, Long Island, where I had spent my summers before entering the seminary. I loved the area, especially the wide open Atlantic Ocean, and the bay, where I went boating. For years, I had been a leader there among a large group of friends my age, but once I began college and then entered the seminary, I noticed my friends' curiosity about my new status, as well as their discomfort with the fact that

I was now different. They showed an exaggerated respect for me as a priest-to-be.

Just as a priest would, I tried to avoid romance. Yet, being a normal, red-blooded teenager, I keenly felt the pull of sexual attraction, so I was careful not to tempt myself beyond what I could handle. I avoided the many beach parties, where drinking and sexual experimentation took place. Still, I remained friendly with everyone, so the group graciously accepted that I was on a different path.

Candidates for a religious community are required to spend a year plus a day in a Novitiate, as an intense introduction to religious life. My father was concerned that I did not understand what embracing celibacy would mean, so for the summer before I entered the Paulist novitiate, he financed a trip to Europe for me. I registered for a two-month tour that began in Brussels and took me through France, Switzerland, Germany, Austria, and Italy. The ancient cities, magnificent cathedrals, Alps, and cultural diversity astounded me. I devoured as much of the culture and sites as possible. On the tour was a vivacious young teacher from Boston. She was only a few years older than me, but she had a joy of life that was infectious. Traveling with her fueled my imagination about what a normal romantic relationship might be like. I had quite a crush on her, so much so that I was strongly tempted to change my plan and not go into the novitiate. But even with the strong pull for sex, I was able to strengthen my resolve to pursue my goal as far as I could. I was not able to put my dad's mind to rest that I had experienced sex, but I did my best to convince him that I felt ready to take the next step toward the priesthood.

The novitiate year began with a weeklong silent retreat led by our novice master, who introduced the group to the monastic rule and the tradition from which it came. His favorite expression was, "Keep the rule and the rule will keep you." For a year, I was steeped in long periods of silence and seclusion in the midst of a vast, wooded tract in central New Jersey. There was no radio, television, or newspaper. One of my jobs was to grade the mile-long dirt road once a week. I would eagerly drive the grader down the hill to the gate at the paved road, shut off the engine, and look out at the world beyond the entrance. I sometimes longed to keep going through the gate back into the familiar world beyond. When I made up my mind that I was not leaving that day, I would restart the engine and drive the grader back to the house. I came to understand that every moment of every day allowed me the chance to renew my commitment.

Fasting, along with extended periods of silence, were regular parts of the novice's life. The monastic routine contributed to an atmosphere of order and stillness. My habit of years as an only child was to carry on an active conversation with my own mind. I analyzed everything. I was a keen observer, analyzing what I saw and heard. I noticed that the solitude bothered some of my fellow novices.

Some of my fellow novices could not tolerate the intensity of the internal exposure that arose from constant silence, and left quickly. In fact, throughout the year, about ten percent of the group who had entered with me slipped away quietly, often without a word to any of us. I found the departures of people to whom I had become close very difficult. The sense of loss triggered my old sense of abandonment and I guarded myself against further losses, holding others at a distance, not knowing who might leave next. As a result, I pulled more into myself. This experience scared me, making intimacy more difficult. I became something of a loner.

I took long walks in the woods every chance I could, exploring nature in every season. The peace that I experienced in nature sustained me whenever the stresses of close living began to grate on my nerves. But because of the rule of silence, I could not resolve conflicts when they came up during the quiet periods. Hurts had to be put on hold until a period when talking was permitted. My self-awareness did not deepen perceptibly. Although my novice master was schooled in religious practices, he did not have a developed understanding of psychology.

On September 8, 1959, I made my first promises of poverty, chastity, and obedience, and was formally inducted into the Paulist community. I was given the Paulist habit, which I would wear daily for the next the years. My mother and father came to St. Paul to witness the investiture ceremony. They were shocked at how thin I was. Afterwards, we drove home to Queens Village together. They could tell there was a difference in me. I found it difficult to make conversation after the year of quiet. My parents had invited my cousins and some friends to their house to welcome me home. But I realized that day that the house in which I had grown up was no longer home to me.

For the next six years, St. Paul's College in Washington, D.C., became my home. There I would live, study, and work. The college was an older, Gothic-style, three-story building with three newer wings. The college provided housing for students, faculty, and a group of Mexican nuns who cooked and did the laundry.

In the college's central wing, a beautiful chapel rose two stories to capture the light. On the floor below was a massive dining hall and kitchen. Other wings held an impressive library with a book bindery attached to it, residences for students and priests, classrooms, and individual small chapels for the priests' private Masses. A central facility was the common room where the students met, watched TV, and debated current issues. All day long, the college hummed with activity and industry.

The life of the college centered on the chapel. Every day, the students and faculty walked into the chapel before dawn to begin the day in prayer. As the voices of the priests and students filled the chapel with Gregorian chant, I felt the sounds deep in my body, and I felt connected to God and my community. We often chanted the Mass in the morning and Vespers in the afternoon. I always looked forward to gathering in the chapel for these communal prayers.

Daily lunches were eaten in silence, during which the students took turns reading aloud to the assembled priests and students. I was a terrible oral reader and dreaded taking my turn. Because of my dyslexia, I compensated by developing a strong memory. The lunch period was usually between a half hour and forty-five minutes, so I would memorize the text I was to read ahead of time, as though it were a role in a play. One day, when it was my turn to read, I began to recite my passage, acting as if I were reading it. All was going well until I mispronounced a place name and the priest in charge asked me to stop reading and read the name again. Of course, I had no idea where I was in the book, and could not reread the name. I was lost. My cover was blown—everyone knew now that I had not been reading at all. It was an awkward and humbling moment for me.

The Paulists are noted for their famous orators. Public speaking, preaching, and radio and TV productions were integral to the work of the community. We were trained to give an extemporary speech and to project our voices into a large hall. The first time I had to stand in front of the class to deliver a three-minute sermon, I was overcome by fear. I stood up but could not utter a word. My kindly professor stopped me and asked me what was the worst thing I could imagine. I told him that I was afraid I would get before the class, forget what I was going to say, and freeze, with everyone laughing at me. The priest said that if I could imagine that, the real experience could only be less. When I rose up again to speak, I completely forgot my opening lines and froze—and everyone in the class laughed good-naturedly. It was a good lesson for me: not to be self-conscious but to communicate with at least one other person. I got over my hesitation eventually and became a persuasive speaker.

Part of the speaking experience was to stand on a soapbox in Lafayette Park in downtown Washington. Lafayette was like Hyde Park in London, where all sorts of speakers would address the people on a Sunday afternoon. As a training experience, we students had to stand up on a speaker's platform in the middle of the park and begin speaking in such a way as to draw a crowd. For me, it was a real jump into the deep end.

The priests who were training me told me they were concerned about the impression I created with my thick Queens accent, which made me sound like the redneck Archie Bunker from the TV show

All in the Family. The priests believed that, sounding the way I did, no one would take me for a well-educated person. I was mortified. As a remedy, I was sent to private speech lessons with a renowned elocution teacher in the drama department at Catholic University. For two years, I learned to open my jaw and my throat, curl my tongue, and form my lips to the shape of vowels and consonants. I was coached several times a week to develop an unaccented speech pattern.

I also learned to open up to other people. When I discovered that my closest friend and classmate at St. Paul's had requested psychological counseling, which the Paulists offered to the students, it came as a complete surprise to me. In the early 1960s, it was unusual to hear of anyone getting professional psychological help. My friend's parents often visited at the same time as mine, and they would often join us on visitors' days. Our parents became friends. When I learned that my friend was in counseling, I became very curious as to why. My friend and I sometimes broke the seminary's no-smoking rule together in the basement of the college. In our smoking hideaway, he confided his suffering, and how the counselor had helped him trace the causes back to his family. My friend acted as if everything in his childhood had been rosy, but as we talked, I realized that was not the case. I also realized that we had a lot in common. I had lived through years of unexpected angry outbursts from my dad. I had to admit to myself that this was also verbal abuse. More seriously, I had lived in dread that my mother was shaping me into her perfect mate, in the image of her father. One of my secrets was that the real reason I had left home during high school was to escape the claustrophobic feeling of being completely smothered by my mother's attention. As an only child, I was the focus of all the tension in my parents' marriage. From listening to my friend's process, I began to gain some self-knowledge. It would take many more years, however, before I would begin to do my own psychological work.

o o o

In the summer of 1960, John F. Kennedy won the Democratic nomination for president. From the day his candidacy was announced at the Democratic convention in Los Angeles to the day an assassin's bullet felled him in Dallas on November 22, 1963, my fellow students and I avidly followed his career. He was the first Catholic to be elected to the White House, and he carried the loyalty of our student body. We cheered aloud in front of the TV set as he debated Richard Nixon during the campaign, and sat up around the clock during the Bay of Pigs Invasion and again during the Cuban Missile Crisis.

Kennedy was the first high-profile liberal Democrat who could enflame the passion of idealism, and set young hearts reaching for a better world. Because of him, I began studying the social teachings of President Franklin D. Roosevelt's New Deal in the 1930s, which saved the United States from the destructive effects of the Depression. Kennedy was philosophically aligned with the political tradition that embodied using state power to improve the lot of everyday people. My father admired FDR's efforts to end the Great Depression. By studying FDR's policies toward unions and the use of state power to curb the banks, I began to understand the similarities between liberal Democratic policy and the social justice teachings of the Catholic Church. I wrote my master's thesis on the parallels between the social justice thinking of Pope John XXIII and the progressive Social Security initiatives of the Roosevelt administration.

Many Catholic homes at that time were decorated with framed photographs of "the two Johns": John F. Kennedy and Pope John XXIII. Eventually, Pope John XXIII would have an even more profound influence on my life than JFK.

When I was growing up, the only Pope I ever knew was Pius XII. He symbolized what many people prized highly: the unchanging nature of the Church. I thought it normal that I would learn my religion from a catechism that was created by the Council of Trent in 1545. My idea of the Church was that it was an institution that had received the divine truth and protected it over the centuries. For me, the Church was infallible in its teachings on faith and morals. If I kept faith with the Church, my salvation was assured.

But on October 9, 1958, during my novitiate year, Pope Pius XII died. I was almost twenty years old, and I felt like I had lost an austere grandfather, a constant and revered presence in my religious consciousness. For the first time in my lifetime, there was going to be an election of a Pope. As novices, we had no access to the news in order to follow the events, but our Novice Master told us that Angelo Giuseppe Roncalli had been elected and had taken the name John XXIII. I was amused by his name choice because the last Pope to choose the name John had served in the 1300s. The new pope's choice of name certainly did not signal that he was very modern, but on that assumption, I would be proven wrong.

In January of 1959, word filtered down to the novices that Pope John XXIII had called an Ecumenical Council, the highest decision-making body in the Catholic Church, and the first one to be convened in over a hundred years. It was a bold move from a Pope who was considered to be an interim caretaker. I wondered what impact this Council would have on me as I entered the major seminary later that year. As it turned out, this event would change my life completely. Pope John XXIII was calling on the Church to reform, and to renew itself.

I had no inkling that the Church needed reform or renewal. My view was that the Church was an unchanging pillar of stability, uninfluenced by the events of the world or the changing social circumstances. What could possibly need to change, I wondered.

o o o

When the Second Vatican Council convened in 1962, I was just beginning my theology studies. I had expected to be studying the textbooks that the Church had been using to train priests since the Council of Trent in the sixteenth century. I watched with fascination as the European and African bishops wrested control from the Vatican bureaucracy. The Papal Curia, the powerful backroom that ruled the Church, had done careful preparatory work. Observers anticipated that the Curia would dominate the Council to insure that little changed, but that was not to be the case.

The amount of change signaled by the work that the new commissions intended to produce was staggering. My astonishment grew during the following sessions. I had not anticipated how much the world's bishops resented the imperious behavior of Rome, and how much they wanted to free up the Church from its effects. Like me, Catholics around the world were closely watching the manoeuvers at Vatican II when, quite unexpectedly, John XXIII died on June 3, 1963. Saddened by the death of this much-loved man I had never met, I wondered what would become of the reforms he had promised at the opening of the Council.

Two weeks after John XXIII passed away, Cardinal Giovanni Battista Enrico Antonio Maria Montini, a close associate of Pope Pius XII, was elected as Pope Paul VI. Montini was closely aligned with the conservative operatives in the papal bureaucracy. I waited to see if Paul VI would cancel the Council and terminate the reform agenda. For me and my colleagues, there was a palpable sense of relief when he announced that the Council would continue, and that he would take a more active role in the Council; but in the end, pressure brought to bear by the world's bishops foretold that the proposed reforms would be debated.

In that crucial time in the Church's history, I aligned myself with the reformers. The theology faculty at St. Paul's decided that we should learn the theology of the Vatican Council. Almost all of my teachers had been students of the leading experts who were researching and writing the Council documents for the bishops. Our professors had access to the draft documents that were being tabled for debate on the floor of the Vatican. St. Paul's faculty decided to put aside the traditional texts that had been used to train seminarians for hundreds of years and use the Council's draft documents to teach us. Hearing the experiences of my teachers and learning of the thinking behind the approach being taken by the majority of the bishops, I became convinced that the reform agenda was needed and would benefit the Church.

I felt privileged to be reviewing the very same documents that the bishops were debating, and felt like I had a front-row seat to the making of history. The emerging theology was evoking deep changes in the Church's thinking, and every day was exciting and uplifting. We anticipated the impact of every reform being proposed to Catholic belief.

Through my teachers' perspective, I understood why the Council was replacing the stagnant, four-hundred-year-old theology with a vibrant and contemporary Christian faith. The renewal embraced the teaching of the great Protestant theologians, as well as Catholic professors who had attained a strong following in Europe. We understood why the document on priestly training placed an emphasis on the necessity of a contemporary understanding of biblical scholarship. Because so much had changed as a result of scholarly advances, it would have been scandalous if students for the priesthood were being taught outmoded scholarship. I could see the negative effects of pastors not knowing the breakthroughs that were being made in scriptural studies. The Church's new position stressed that any doctrinal teaching had to be set in the context of sound scriptural scholarship.

As I studied the New Testament, my eyes were opened by how some of the world's greatest scholars had deconstructed the Gospels, peeling back historic additions to uncover the oldest layer: the words of Jesus. In my scriptural studies classes, everything I had learned in my parochial school about the Bible was being transformed. Each of the Gospels had been compiled over time by several authors, who each relied upon a source document—likely containing a collection of the sayings of Jesus—that was no longer in existence. Each author had a different intent and a different audience to whom he was writing. My early religious education had not given me any preparation for the revelations that were part of my training in biblical studies.

Gently, my biblical studies professor led us into the world of modern biblical interpretation. We studied books that had been written on the Bible following World War II. The same code-breaking skills that had been used to decipher wartime communication were now being used to crack Egyptian hieroglyphics and biblical languages. Archeology was uncovering civilizations that shed new light on the history of the Middle East, and the Bible ceased being the only window to the ancient era. Textual criticism was improving scholars' ability to trace the development of ideas in the various biblical versions. I was surprised that there were no versions of the Old Testament available from the time the books were written. The oldest texts date from the second and third centuries, much later than I had once assumed.

o o o

I was first introduced to the way that the ancient world imagined the universe, the oldest cosmology, as I studied the Bible, and I learned that all of the world religions share the same cosmological assumptions. I began to understand that in order to interpret a particular book of the Bible, I had to appreciate the way the author thought. I discovered that the Bible is a literary work with styles and ways of speaking which have been lost over time. My scripture classes were exciting, and I overflowed with new knowledge. I also discovered that when I tried to tell my family about these new insights, they were aghast, not wanting their faith disturbed.

Even in the seminary, I recognized that the biggest challenge for theologians was the Doctrine of Original Sin. St. Augustine, who lived five hundred years after the time of Christ, invented the concept of an Original Sin as a way to explain his own propensity to sin. The literal interpretation of the book of Genesis, with its story of Adam and Eve disobeying a divine order, fit St. Augustine's search. However, in order to use the story, he needed it to be literally true. So St. Augustine persuaded his fellow bishops that everyone in the Church needed to believe that the first parents' sin against God infected all of humanity with a primal state of sinfulness. The Early Church had also adopted his thesis that the Bible had to be interpreted literally. Now scholars knew that the Bible's authors had never intended to say that Adam and Eve in the Garden of Eden were real.

When I first learned about this, I was so shocked that I needed to talk with the priest who was my teacher. What was emerging from my study of the Bible was a picture that contradicted one of the basic tenets of Christianity: Original Sin. It also removed the central reason that the Church used to explain why Jesus died: to redeem the world from sin.

I was shaken. For thousands of years, the Church had explained the mystery of salvation based on a misinterpretation of the Bible. The heavy emphasis on sin—so present in the Christian preaching and teaching that had shaped my thinking and my own beliefs—was the invention of fourth-century teachers and not at all authentic to the original meaning of the author of Genesis. I also realized that if the more authentic meaning were to become known, it would take the Church in a very different direction. It would place the emphasis on Jesus's teaching of love, not on sin and evil. I was thoroughly exhilarated by this idea.

We theology students, who now knew there was no basis for reading the Garden story literally, could look to science to explore whether mankind is evolving and if there had been a perfect state in the beginning, from which we had fallen, as the Bible seemed to assume. Homo sapiens emerged around two hundred thousand years ago. According to the vast array of contemporary fossil records, the world has been evolving in a progressive direction, from a more primitive state to a more diverse and developed condition. It did not begin in perfect state that went downhill. There could not have been a literal Garden of Eden, and there was certainly no first couple whose descendants generated all other humans. However, even a hundred years ago, before Darwin, this was not known.

The excitement of uncovering this new information, with its earthshattering implications, was hard to contain. If there was no Garden of Eden, and no Adam and Eve, then there could never have been an Original Sin. The Church would have to admit that its view of humanity as fallen and mired in an inherited sin needed to change. I felt like a new dawn was breaking that would bring fresh light to my work as a teacher.

I wanted the opportunity to discard the emphasis that sin and guilt played at the center of the Church's view of humanity, and I thought that others would welcome this change too. I saw the message of love replacing the emphasis on hell and damnation. The way I saw it, here was an ideal opportunity for the Church to re-articulate the role of Jesus in history, and to end its fixation on sin and sex.

There were other changes coming out of the Vatican Council about the formation of priests that I also wanted to promote. As the elected leader of the students, I met with our rector and proposed that we form a council to adopt some of the recommendations in the Vatican Council document on priestly training. He agreed, and we created a forum that we called *Aggiornamento*, after the word Pope John XXIII used, which mean "bringing up to date." We used the draft document on priestly training as a template. The outcome was that we Paulist seminarians in the Washington, D.C., area were mandated to engage in supervised pastoral activity.

This was a departure from the model that had been in place for centuries. Up until then, those wo were studying to become priests were separated from the real world around them. I thought that our seminary had taken a bold new step.

I chose a parish in the heart of Washington's black ghetto. I worked under Father Geno Baroni, a charismatic local pastor. One of my first activities was to ensure that all of the children in the neighborhood were given the new polio vaccine. My work involved visiting a list of houses on a particular block, going to to door to hand out information about getting children to the clinic. But I could not find one of the families on the list. When I asked the kids on the street if they could tell me where to find the family, they led me under a front stoop into a bunker that ran the length of the house above. The ends of the hall were boarded up, with a door at the front end. In this long, single room the kitchen, eating and sleeping areas were all open to each other. There was the woman I was looking for. She had seven young children living in that space. I was sickened to find these Third World conditions, and when I reacted to how hard it must be to live under such conditions, the woman agreed and told me about having to stay up all night to keep rats away from the children.

In the early 1960s, U.S. laws still permitted segregation, and surely there was no better example of its wretched effects than this bunker. Because African Americans were denied housing in the surrounding states, they were forced to find accommodation within the Washington, D.C., city limits. It didn't matter if an African American person was a well-educated civil servant who had come to work for the Kennedy administration or a poor migrant recently arrived from the South—both were confined to the limited housing available in Washington, where housing prices were exorbitant and rental housing conditions were very poor.

As if that wasn't bad enough, one major supermarket had a practice of shipping its day-old produce from the suburban stores into the central city ones so that the inner-city African American residents never saw fresh food. Father Geno encouraged us to bring the radical social organizer Saul Alinski to the parish to teach us how to mobilize the residents who were yearning for change. We used Alinski's book *Rules for Radicals* to run workshops for people who wanted to advocate for social change in the inner city.

Because of my exposure to the living conditions in the inner city, I wanted to take action against segregation and racial injustice. It was not enough for me to study the Bible. I realized that social action was also part of my spiritual calling. The day the U.S. Congress began to debate the *Civil Rights Act* I had assembled a large contingent of seminarians, divinity students, and nuns willing to devote several hours a week to staff a silent vigil in front of the Lincoln Memorial. We took up prominent positions in front of the statue of Abraham Lincoln, which looks up the Washington Mall at the United States Capital. To my amazement, an equally large contingent of brown-shirted Neo-Nazis, dressed in full uniform, set up a counter demonstration facing us. A reporter from *LIFE*, noting the highly charged atmosphere, said I could make the cover of *LIFE* if I went up to the Neo-Nazis and got into an argument with them. But since we had disciplined our group to be silent and nonviolent, I declined.

That evening, a car pulled up near the demonstration line and a tall black man got out and approached the vigil. He asked who was in charge, and I identified myself. He wanted us to know how much our support meant to the civil rights struggle. He introduced himself as Reverend Martin Luther King. I knew that we were protesting in the very place from which he had addressed hundreds of thousands of supporters and delivered his call for a new day of integration. He was one of the leaders I most admired in that era. I had followed and esteemed his commitment to nonviolent action to change hearts about anti-black prejudice for years. As I trained to become a priest, I drew on the qualities that King and Beroni modeled.

I was combining my cutting-edge studies with social activism, the two pillars of my view of the ideal way to live the priesthood. In the early 1960s, it seemed that goodwill and hard work could

change the world. Politics and renewal theology combined to produce change in both the religious and secular realms. At that time,
I believed that religion was an instrument for the betterment of
the world, and I was readying myself to take a leading role in the
Church's renewal.

2

Thou Art a Priest Forever

The source is within you,
And this whole world is springing up from it.
The source is full,
And its waters are ever-flowing.
Do not grieve, drink your fill.
Don't think it will ever run dry, this endless ocean.

—Rumi

I SLEPT VERY little the night before my ordination. The magnitude of the step I was about to take loomed large. *How was it that I was called to the priesthood?* I realized how completely set apart a priest's life is. There would never be a moment when I was not a priest in the eyes of the churched or the unchurched. There would always be camaraderie, but little deep companionship or intimacy. Besides, there would be no children in my future, and my family genes would end with me. A specter of solitary life awaited me.

The next morning, on ordination day, May 8, 1965, four of us from the original class of about twenty-seven knelt before Cardinal Spellman to hear him say the words of St. Paul's epistle: "Thou

art a priest forever according to the order of Melchizedek." We all
had gone through the same struggles and doubts, the same training
and encouragement. It is hard for anyone outside the mythos of
Catholicism to understand my awe of becoming a priest. Culturally,
a priest was a person of influence and often held significant power
in Catholic communities. But it wasn't the authority of the priesthood that appealed to me. It was the intermediary role of bringing
divine blessing to the believing community. Within the religious
culture of the 1960s, the priesthood was considered a position of
great honor. My novice master often held up the idealized nature
of the role before me. He would often recite this saying from Jean-
Baptiste Henri Lacordaire, OP, an activist priest who reestablished
the Dominican Order in post-Revolutionary France:

> To live in the midst of the world with no desire for its
> pleasures; to be a member of every family, yet belonging
> to none; to share all sufferings; to penetrate all secrets,
> to heal all wounds; to go daily from men to God to
> offer Him their homage and petitions; to return from
> God to men to bring them His pardon and hope; to
> have a heart of fire for charity and a heart of bronze for
> chastity; to bless and to be blest forever. O God, what a
> life, and it is yours, O Priest of Jesus Christ!

What kind of priest I would be? I wanted to embody these characteristics and be an admirable priest, an image of Christ in these
times.

Most of my ordination day is a blur, except for my parents being there and two segments of the ceremony. The first segment was having my hands anointed by Cardinal Spellman and then having them wrapped in white linen. The other is my memory of lying face down on the cold marble floor of the Church of St. Paul the Apostle. Father Isaac Hecker, the founder of the Paulists, is buried in the church, and thoughts of him came to me as I lay there. After ten years of preparation, I was filled with the realization I was now a priest.

I so clearly remember my mother and father being there. My mother, Alice, who wore in her finest dress and a fur stole, could not have been more proud. If she had been going to visit the Queen of England, she could not have been better dressed. Tears dampened her soft, radiant face behind the scholarly glasses she always wore.

Next to my mother, my grandmother, Agnes, the other most significant woman in my early life, was also dressed in her finest, though her style was of a much earlier generation. Agnes was the matriarch of the O'Donnell clan, which included my mother, and a large woman in every way. Her adult children always deferred to her, and she dominated their lives just as she dominated any gathering with her dynamic presence. She loved her grandchildren unconditionally, and I always felt special and beloved when I was with her. In fact, Agnes had saved my life when I was a very young child and became anemic. The doctor believed I might not survive without constant love and attention, so my grandmother came to live in our house to nurture me back to health. She held the prophecy of my grandfather, that I would be the first American pope, in her heart, and I believe she always knew I would be a priest.

My dad, Jack, was a hardworking steam fitter. As a construction worker, he installed heating and refrigeration units in the skyscrapers that were sprouting up throughout Manhattan. He had great difficulty articulating his love and pride, but it shone on his face that day. He had often urged me to get an education. "It is easier to earn a living with your head than with your hands," he would say. He had trained me to be good with my hands, but not to follow in his footsteps; he inspired me with his example of hard work and his craftsman's sense of what constituted a good job.

Dad had been orphaned as a boy, and I knew next to nothing about his parents or their families. He was twelve when his mother died, leaving him and his brother and sister to be raised by cousins. He never spoke much about the people who raised him, and he was very protective of his feelings. Dad had difficult expressing his love for me, but he was always affectionate toward me. Although he could be verbally abusive and was a harsh taskmaster, I never doubted that he loved me.

During the Great Depression, my father was forced to abandon his dream of becoming an engineer when he left school at the urging of his brother and sister to manage the apartment building that his mother had inherited and left to her own family. But the building failed when the tenants could not pay the rent, and with it went Dad's hopes for a share of the American Dream.

My mother was my most important influence. I loved her as the sunflower loves the sun, but our relationship was intense and complicated. Though I don't remember much about my toddler years, I do have a memory of my mother leaving our apartment in the Bronx. She was a teacher and returned to work when I was about two. It felt like I was being abandoned and the experience

33

imprinted deeply in my psyche. My reaction was to stop eating, so that, slowly, over the next year or so, I became anemic and began to fade away. The doctor called it "failure to thrive," though I was most likely grieving for the loss of the closeness of my mother.

That was when my grandmother came to live with us. We had moved into a new house in Queens Village that my father had renovated for us. Agnes nurtured me, loving and feeding me back to vitality. My mother also gave up teaching to stay home with me. Although I could not have understood it then, she became anxious and fearful, believing she had failed me. She gave me such constant attention that I too became fearful and insecure. However, by the time I was in school I had become her confidant, spending many hours talking with her, as though I was another adult.

Now, as a new priest, being with my family and our wide circle of friends swelled my heart. I knew that I was fulfilling their dream as much as my own. Being a priest in an Irish Catholic family was both an honor and a new level of responsibility. As I drove home after the ordination with my grandmother and parents, I believed I was different, that somehow the ordination had changed me.

My few days at home were strange. I was overwhelmed by everyone's adulation. My adult relatives would genuflect before me and ask to be blessed. Friends from childhood would kneel and ask, "May I have your blessing, Father?"

But I only had a few days at home before I would head to my first assignment, in Vancouver, Canada. I would go by way of Saskatoon. I entered Canada by way of Toronto. As I came through Customs and Immigration, I applied for Landed Immigrant status, believing that I would be in Canada for a long time. I would have loved to continue working in an inner city, ministering to the poor, but my superiors said that they had rained me to teach the new theology, which was far more needed from me than urban ministry.

In Vancouver, I was to help establish a Catholic information center. I was looking forward to it, because I thought it would be the perfect opportunity for me to teach other people what I had been learning. I was also excited about living and working in Western Canada, which was a new world for me. During the previous summer, I had worked at the Catholic Center in Toronto with a man called Ed Bader, who was to be my partner in Vancouver. Ed had already hired a woman named Madeleine Longo, who was well regarded among Catholic Center workers across the country for establishing the centers in Saskatoon and in Calgary, where she had been the lay director.

o o o

Ed recommended that I stop in Saskatoon to attend a national meeting of the Catholic Center directors. It was a wonderful opportunity to mix with the priests and lay men and women who were working at the centers. I was welcomed warmly at a spaghetti and meatball feast that Madeleine had cooked for the thirty or so people at the conference.

My job would be to develop religious education programs for adults—for people who were seeking to become Catholics as well as Catholics who wanted more information about the new teaching from Vatican II. Archbishop Johnson, who had invited the Paulists to Vancouver, wanted us to begin with instruction in Catholicism for inquirers. The Paulists had developed an introduction to the Catholic faith based on the way inquirers had been taught during the earliest days of the Church. I was eager to recruit volunteers to be co-instructors with me. This was also an innovation that had been developed by the Paulists in Toronto, where it had attracted substantial numbers of people. This approach would introduce me to lay people in Vancouver, many of whom became my close friends. I was excited about beginning my new work as a priest.

Madeleine and I conceived an introductory series of talks on Vatican II by prominent Catholic participants at Simon Fraser University. The Vatican II talks consistently drew large, paying audiences. Consequently, I spoke to pastors from parishes in key areas of the city and asked them to invite Center staff to deliver a ten-week course in their parishes. In every location, people fully subscribed to the series.

But not long after the series began, I started to receive negative feedback from local clergy. Their comments set up red flags that I foolishly ignored. While the laity loved the content of my course on the renewal of Catholicism, the pastors were aghast at what they were hearing about the course from their parishioners, who talked enthusiastically about the new theology. Few of priests had even read anything about the new thinking. They had been schooled in the pre-Vatican Council approach, and Archbishop Johnson had not brought the renewal home with him from Rome. Because I was a newly ordained priest, I never thought to offer an introductory course for the clergy.

Only a handful of the younger priests had been keeping abreast of the new theology, and the others considered them radical. Many local priests were quite alarmed by the changes from the Council. They had been trained to the way of thinking that the Council hoped to change, and most of them were unprepared to investigate the new direction, much less adopt the new theology. They considered the new ideas dangerous. Many even outright rejected all the changes, including celebrating Mass in English, facing the people.

By then I was actively implementing the changes wherever I could. I abandoned the closed confessional and welcomed people to an office-like setting. The rote "Bless me, Father, for I have sinned," was replaced by a face-to-face acknowledgment of the consequences of the behavior. If someone was stealing from his employer, he could not get away with "I broke the eighth commandment." When we talked about what he was doing, he understood that he had to stop and begin making restitution. I would ask the person who came in to confess having committed adultery against his wife to think about what the consequences would be if he had an affair with someone who was already married. Most of the people who came to confession in this way told me how much more meaningful their experience was. This feedback confirmed for me why the Council had made that change. I felt like I was an instrument of moral change.

I was a regular panelist on an open-line call-in radio program called "God Talk," which started up in Vancouver while I was there. The show was hosted by United Church minister Roy Bonisteel, and featured Walter Donald from the Anglican Church and me. We drew a large listening audience for a Sunday morning. The lively interchange among us was interesting and sometimes irreverent, but also informative and relevant. The audience loved it.

Monsignor James Carney was named bishop the second year I was in Vancouver. He was one of the pastors who opposed my work, and openly expressed his opinion that I was dangerous. His knowledge of Vatican II was minimal, and he proclaimed himself a conservative defender of the pre-Council faith. A few months after he became bishop, he called me into his office to tell me he had put in a request to the Paulists to remove me from his archdiocese. I felt like I had been slapped in the face. I believed in what I was doing, and could not fathom why a bishop would reject me for doing it. I took Bishop Carney's rejection personally, and was humiliated by it, especially in the face of the community of lay people with whom I worked.

Soon after my meeting with Bishop Carney, I contacted the Bishop of Victoria, Remi DeRoo, and asked him if I could work for him. He was known to be a champion of Vatican II and a promoter of adult religious education. He suggested that I talk with my order and get their reaction to my plan. We agreed to meet at a theology conference in Montreal later that month. However, when I got there, he told he had had decided it would not be a good idea for me to come to work for him.

It was wrenching to leave the work and the friends I had developed in Vancouver, and to be blackballed in my first assignment was chilling. But in early September 1967, I reported to the Paulist parish at the University of Texas in Austin. I had accepted an invitation from Father Walter Dalton, who had called to ask me to come work with him. He told me he was aware of what I had done in Vancouver and wanted me to do the same work at the university parish. Walter had a reputation among the Paulists as a wise and kind pastor, and he wanted to bring Vatican II reforms to his parish. Instead of being exiled from Vancouver, I was being given an opportunity not only to teach about the changes in the Church, but also to implement them in a parish setting. Because of the university setting, the parish attracted many young, well-educated families who were curious about the Church's much-publicized reforms.

I had Father Dalton's backing. He announced to the parish that I was St. Austin's new director of religious education, and asked me to enliven the Masses and integrate the changes mandated by the Council into the life of the parish. The first thing I did was to dedicate one Sunday Mass to young families. I recruited an advisory group of parishioners to help me. Among those people was a talented musician who attracted guitarists and singers to the parish. We brought in guitars, flutes, and drums, and began to play progressive religious folk music. The group selected lively songs and taught a group of young singers to perform the repertoire. The altar already had been turned to face the people, but I located it lower and closer to the people so that it was more easily visible. I spoke the words of the celebration with meaning. The homilies drew on the modern biblical understanding, showing how the Gospels evolved in the context of the early Christian community. Often we would hold a discussion among the people attending, asking those present to relate the scriptural reading to some aspect of their lives. After the service, I initiated a drop-in with refreshments and a chance for people to discuss local issues.

Other Masses in the parish were also tuned to the people who usually attended. The goal was to make the experience of worship as relevant as possible. Word spread, and people began coming from other areas to participate in our services.

I volunteered as a literacy teacher, and recruited other parishioners to become involved. Blacks and Hispanic migrants who lived in the parish were often hampered in their employment by a lack of literacy. My first client, an older woman, expressed radiant joy when she learned to write her name. She brought in her children and grandchildren to watch her fulfill this lifelong aspiration.

Austin City Council had a bylaw that allowed segregated housing. With a group of men from the parish, I took a leading role in a political campaign to overturn the bylaw. The local real estate industry and some businesses objected, sponsoring a full-page ad in Austin's daily newspaper naming the campaign's organizers as troublemakers. I was happy to be on that list.

The parish committee that was responsible for teaching religion to public school children came under my responsibility as director of religious education. One evening, they began talking about the Gospels during our meeting. After listening for a while, I began to introduce them to some of the things I had learned about the Gospels. We looked at when they were written, who the audience was, and, consequently, what the author was teaching. That the Gospels were not histories or journalism, or even eyewitness accounts came as a revelation to the children.

The committee members were riveted by thinking about how long after Jesus's death the Gospels had been composed. We looked at why the Gospels had been written, and for whom. Why was one account so different from the other three? I got them to read the newly discovered Gospel of Thomas and to imagine why it had not been included with the others. The committee members could not get enough. I began to regain confidence that the new discoveries were relevant to maturing spirituality.

I had opened the door to adult religious education. The committee members began to ask about the program I had created in Vancouver. When I told them, including that I had partnered with a laywoman in creating and delivering the program, they immediately wanted to bring her to Austin. After getting Father Walter Dalton's blessing, they invited Madeleine Longo to come to Austin for an interview. The parishioners were impressed by her, and decided to hire her to work in the education program for the parish.

When Madeleine joined the parish staff, we were able to mount a program that addressed elementary and high school students as well as adults. The adult series deconstructed the Catechism—the basic question-and-answer book, developed four hundred years earlier to combat the Protestant Reformation, that is now used in every parochial elementary school to teach Catholicism. The Catechism fosters an infantile stance in the learner. Most of the adults who had attended parochial school had never updated their juvenile understanding of their faith. The course introduced spirituality as an adult experience of inner awareness of the transcendent. To deepen the religious experience of the committee, I began to accept invitations to celebrate Mass in their homes, showing them how the earliest liturgy developed in the homes of the first Christians.

Two events occurred my second year in Austin that changed the future course of my life, and Pope Paul VI was responsible for both. He had presided over the end of the Vatican Council, and was known to have opposed the direction that the bishops had adopted.

41

Three years after the close of the Council, I heard that he intended to issue a new creed, and I could not wait to read what he was going to propose. I worried that it was too soon, since the theologians had not had much discussion about how to shift the Church from its preoccupation with sin and sex to Christ's message of love. And when I obtained a copy of the Pope's new creed, I could not believe what I read. The *Credo of the People of God* rejected every insight that had emerged at the Council. It went back to the fourth century and reiterated the position of the first ecumenical council at Nicea. In order to believe the statements in the creed, a contemporary Christian would have to accept the worldview that had been abandoned four hundred years ago. It was insulting to everyone who had tried to bring Catholic belief into the twentieth century.

In the prologue, the Pope said he was aware of the pressures that were bubbling to the surface throughout the Church, questioning the traditional formulation of the Christian faith, and he wished to reaffirm the archaic formulation of the fourth century. I could sense the energy being sucked out of the spirit of renewal in the Church. The Pope was using his full authority to nullify the work of the bishops of the Council.

I was particularly disturbed by the way he contradicted the scholarly evidence about the Bible. I could just imagine the conservative Curia working on him for the past three years to turn back the clock to the days before Pope John. He made his reason clear: "The greatest care must be taken, while fulfilling the indispensable duty of research, *to do no injury to the teaching of Christian doctrine* [emphasis added]. For that would be to give rise, as is unfortunately seen in these days, to disturbance and perplexity in many faithful souls."[1]

At the time, I thought the Pope and his shadowy advisors must have panicked when they saw the extent of what the Council had endorsed. I could see them saying, "But Holy Father, we cannot admit that we were not infallible. We used to teach that we had the eternal truth. How can we possibly admit now that we did not know the full truth? You have to reassure people and persuade them that nothing has changed."

I could see their dilemma. If they admitted that new information has come to light that added to the way that those who lived fifteen hundred years ago saw things, what would that say about the declaration that the Church is infallible? Having formally claimed that the Church could not make a mistake, how could it admit that they had been wrong? They would have had to humbly admit that what they taught needed to change. Rather than admitting that, just as in every other area of human understanding, new learning had added to our knowledge, they tried to say that the fourth century church had all the answers, and said everything appropriately. Surely, Christians could accept that fourth century bishops had put their best effort into articulating the beliefs, and could now acknowledge that newer and clearer understanding had emerged. But I could see what had happened. Because the new information had eclipsed their worldview, the Vatican advisors had convinced the Pope to pretend that nothing had changed.

[1] Pope Paul VI, "The Credo of the People of God", Proclaimed June 30, 1968 http://www.ewtn.com/library/papaldoc/p6credo.htm

It did not seem to matter to him that the old views were not believable in the light of contemporary knowledge. In order to avoid "disturbance and perplexity in many faithful souls," Pope Paul VI consciously turned his back on the modern worldview and what had been discovered about the Bible. By opting to cling to a perspective from the days when the Earth was believed to be flat and heaven was a physical place up above the dome of the sky, the Pope guaranteed that the faith he proclaimed would remain unbelievable. I was irate that, in his rejection of present knowledge of the Bible and the contemporary, scientific understanding of the universe, the Pope was engaging in willful ignorance. He denied almost all of the development of knowledge over the past two thousand years. By doing so, he engaged in what can only be described as a cover-up, rejecting scholarship and truth in favor of protecting the faithful and keeping church members in ignorance. He was sweeping knowledge and science under the rug, creating a crisis for everyone who had just watched the Vatican Council commit the Church to the pursuit of sound biblical scholarship.

Why did this matter so much to me? Many of my priest associates saw what I saw, but elected to ignore it, telling themselves they could pick and choose which things the Pope taught them to accept. They advised me to ignore the *Credo*. But I could not do that. The Council's vote to embrace the new understanding of the role of the Bible was overwhelming in favor of what the Pope was now ignoring.

o o o

How could I deny the similarity of this decision to the previous condemnation of Galileo for saying that the sun, not the Earth, was the center of the solar system? Or to the rejection of Charles Darwin's findings on evolution?

Disheartened, to put it mildly, I awaited the outcry that I was sure would come from bishops around the world, but there was only silence. Where had the collective will of the Church gone? What had happened to my Church in so few years, from the end of the Council to this assertion of belief statements that were so patently false?

Less than a month later, Pope Paul issued an Encyclical letter that had a crushing effect on millions of men and women awaiting the update of its position on the birth control pill. *Humanae vitae* (human life) was even more devastating to lay Catholics than the Creed. The Pope condemned the use of the pill and all birth control methods except for abstinence. He overruled the scientific evaluation of the birth control pill and rejected the unanimous decision of the lay and clerical members of his own papal commission, both of which found the birth control pill acceptable. The anguish of Catholic couples was tangible. I heard Confession from many women as well as men who were at the point of despair over the banning of all forms of birth control.

For a church that was charged with ensuring its members' moral wellbeing, denying access to a safe and legal contraception that met all the criteria of acceptability made no sense. Our local bishop instructed all of the parishes to read a statement he issued obliging Catholics to follow the Pope's guidance, and the parish priests discussed how to respond to this grim position. We all understood that this announcement put married people in an untenable position, and we felt that we had an obligation to give them some guidance to put the papal edict in context.

I suggested that we remind the people of the language on freedom of conscience that had been issued by the Vatican Council. Father Dalton asked me to preach the homily at all of the Masses on the Sunday following the Pope's announcement. I read the bishop's letter that demanded that all Catholics accept the Pope's decision. I then read the opening lines of the Declaration on Religious Freedom from the Documents of Vatican Council II, 1966:

> A sense of the dignity of the human person has been impressing itself more and more deeply on the consciousness of contemporary man. And the demand is increasingly made that men should act on their own judgment, enjoying and making use of a responsible freedom, not driven by coercion but motivated by a sense of duty.[2]

I ended with the definition of conscience from the Church in the Modern World:

> Conscience is the most secret core and sanctuary of man. There he is alone with God, whose voice echoes in the depths. In a wonderful manner, conscience reveals that law which is fulfilled by love of God and neighbor.

[2] Documents of Vatican Council II, 1966, n., 675.

> In fidelity to conscience, Christians are joined with the
> rest of men in the search for truth, and for the genuine
> solution to the numerous problems which arise in the
> life of individuals and from social relationships.[3]

I ended by reminding the congregation of the language endorsed by the Vatican Council on freedom of conscience. Conscientious people had the right to make their own moral decisions, and did not need to simply obey someone else's judgments. Some people actually began to weep with relief during the sermon. Whatever consequences would fall on me, I knew that I had eased the conscience of the congregation at St. Austin's.

First thing Monday morning, the phone rang in the pastor's office. The bishop ordered Father Walter Dalton and me to appear in his office the next day. When we arrived, he was livid. Walter had never seen him so angry. The bishop accused us of defying him. He interpreted what we had done as an act of insubordination and a disregard of his authority. Nothing we could say about what we intended would abate his temper. He ended his tirade by saying that he was temped to expel the Paulists from the diocese.

It was beyond question that the initiative of Pope John XXIII was dead. The back-room papal bureaucrats who wanted to quash the spirit and content of Vatican II had won. A short time later, the Vatican began to silence Council's theologians. Those who were the

[3] Vatican Council II, W.M. Abbott (S.J.) (Ed.) *The documents of Vatican II*. New York: Herder & Herder, 1966.

major influences at the Council were removed from their teaching positions at Catholic universities. I saw the writing on the wall.

A year later, it was my turn to be silenced. Father Walter Dalton was transferred to a new parish, and the new pastor who replaced him had not been in the job long when a contingent of wealthy parishioners pressured him to end the adult religious education program for teaching ideas that they found foreign. They wanted me removed from both teaching and preaching. It was heartbreaking to watch the new pastor knuckle under. He had no idea of the renewal that had taken place in the parish, or the role that the Council teaching had played in it.

My retrenchment destroyed my belief in the Church and shattered my sense of spirituality. Instead of representing a church that was coming up to date, I was being confronted by deceit and a cover-up. Rather than do the work of renewal, the Church's leadership preferred to teach a formula that was out of place in the twentieth century. I realized that all the training I'd had, all the deepening to an adult Christianity, and all the credibility I had put into helping my course participants trust the renewal was wasted.

I could no longer trust the Church. The Pope and his closest Cardinals were perpetrating a fraud. The Church's credibility was gone, and with it, my faith in everything I had been taught about religion.

Ironically, it was Holy Week when the Paulists at St. Austin's decided that I should be reassigned to hospital and convent chaplaincy. I was not to teach or preach at parish Masses anymore. At that point, I decided that I could not stay. On Holy Thursday, I packed my bag with the few clothes I owned, and left Austin. As a Paulist,

I was given $30 spending money each month. My promise to live a life of personal poverty meant that my community took care of my basic needs, but I had nothing of my own. I had no savings, and no credit card in my own name. I had no way to leave without borrowing money.

I had to ask my dad for enough money to buy a car. When I told him what had happened to me, he immediately got me the money. I was alone and in pain, and had no idea where to go, so, instinctively, I headed to my parents' house on Long Island. I arrived feeling utterly defeated. My faith was in tatters and I had headed back to my childhood home as a refuge. I was thirty-one, and had not lived with my parents for twelve years or seen them since my ordination. They had retired to a new house they had built in Southampton and welcomed me without question.

I was a priest without a church. My relationship with the Church had failed, but I believed that my church had left me and not the other way around. Everything I had worked for was gone. The life to which I had committed myself no longer existed. I had no idea what life held for me. I was numb, confused, and ill prepared for whatever would come next.

My mother could feel my deep suffering, and yet, I could not explain my distress to her. Her lifetime of piety and devotion predisposed her to trust the Church. I did not want to tell her how the Church was betraying her. At the same time, she was upset by the degree of turmoil that I was going through. My dad somehow knew, without me spelling it out, that I had left the Paulists. In his own silent way, he simply accepted me, without needing to understand why I had left, and was glad to have me home.

Day after day, that chilly spring, I walked along the empty shoreline of the Atlantic Ocean. The gunmetal sky of April reflected my dark interior landscape. I got in touch with how angry I was. I bridled at the betrayal of the conservative power block in the church to frustrate the will of the majority of Council bishops. Most of all I felt hurt and personally betrayed.

Toward the end of the month, I called the Paulists headquarters in Scarsdale, New York, to make an appointment to see Father John Fitzgerald, the president of the Paulists. I knew that John had been to Austin to mediate a dispute between the new pastor, Ed Pietrucha, and a group of parishioners who were outraged about his decision to cancel the religious education program. I hoped that John had learned a great deal about the value of the work I was doing, but I also worried that, as an old-school priest, he might judge me as responsible for the dispute, and not help heal the rift. When I drove up to see him, I was told that he was away, and referred to his assistant.

My conversation with John's deputy was very discouraging. This man did not know me at all. He read from my record, which showed that I had been removed from Vancouver at the request of the bishop, and that I had been at the center of a dispute in Austin. I felt invisible, and like I was talking to a stone wall. I needed a kindly shepherd who would understand my need for refuge, even if I did not see that myself. Sitting in John's formal study, which seemed designed to convey his power, I did not find the humanity I was looking for. The coldness of that interview left me feeling like an alien.

I returned to Long Island and began contemplating what to do next. I felt a terrible animosity, and not just to the Pope. He was the leader of a church that had set out to reform itself, but he had wound up revealing a duplicity that scandalized me. I could not see myself continuing to serve the Church as a priest.

I realized with a heavy heart that my career as a priest was truly over. I needed to leave the priesthood for my mental health and integrity. The Church has a formal procedure for priests who want to leave, which involves petitioning the Pope for a dispensation from the vows of celibacy and renouncing any future exercise of the priesthood. I had heard that it was quite a lengthy process and would involve appearing before three judges from the Curia. The process requires that a petitioner prove that he made a mistake in becoming a priest in the first place. Usually the underlying assumption is that the priest wants to get married. But I did not believe that I had made a mistake in becoming a priest. In fact, I still thought I was a good and effective priest.

I was most angry at the Church for pretending that it had not recently discovered that many of its doctrines were not based on fact. The combination of the limitations of the ancient worldview, together with the significance of the new discoveries, made it impossible for me to cling to outmoded beliefs. Because the Church had declared itself infallible, incapable of making an error, it was now was too embarrassed to admit it had been were misinformed. I found this outrageous.

The early Church fathers had no way of knowing what seminary students of the Bible know today. The latest information about the Bible, which had resulted from discoveries made in the past seventy-five years, simply was not available in the third century. It had only become available due to archeological and other modern scientific breakthroughs. Usually, the human response to any new knowledge available is to admit it and begin to incorporate it.

With each day, my decision to leave the clergy was gradually strengthened. I realized it was time to tell my mother and father that I had decided to leave the priesthood. Not surprisingly, my parents responded very differently to the news. My dad was supportive, even secretly glad that I was rejoining the world and would be able to enjoy a more normal life. My mother, on the other hand, was very upset. That didn't surprise me because my decision meant the end of her dream of having a priest for a son. What did surprise me was that, in the absence of information about my inner struggle with the Church, my mother assumed that my teaching partner, Madeleine Longo, had lured me away from my vows. The thought had never entered my mind. Nonetheless, my mom was convinced that I was leaving to get married.

She also assumed that I would settle somewhere close to her. If I was not going to be a priest anymore, then the least I could do would be to live close enough for her to see me regularly. But that was not in my plan either. Since my teenage years, my relationship with my mother had left me feeling smothered. I knew that I needed to live at a distance so that I was not pulled under by her emotional domination. I loved both of my parents, but I was sure that I could not live near them. When I told my mom that I probably would go out West, she simply began to cry. Her reaction broke my heart, but I knew that it was time for me to leave.

3

The Painful Walk to Freedom

*But little by little, as you left their voices behind, the stars
began to burn through the sheets of clouds, and there was
a new voice which you slowly recognized as your own, that
kept you company as you strode deeper and deeper into the
world, determined to do the only thing you could do, determined to save the only life you could save.*

—Mary Oliver

I HAD SO many questions, in the days after I decided to leave the
priesthood. I was beset by fear and uncertainty. How was I going
to support myself and make a living? I'd had no reason to ask that
question during the dozen years I spent in the religious community.
Everything I needed had been provided for me by the generosity
of others. Those who contributed to the collection plate at Sunday
Mass or gave to support the Paulists contributed to my upkeep. I
lived then in a state of perpetual dependency. Now the harsh reality
sank in: I would have to grow up and provide for myself.

I had no marketable skills. Of what commercial value was a
degree in theology? Through my years of specialized study within

the Church, I had never held a job in the world. Several more years of school would be required to qualify myself to teach religious studies, and I had no way of financing that kind of program. Besides, I was far from sure that I even wanted to teach anything about religion.

∘ ∘ ∘

I had no confidence in my ability to survive in the secular world. Living my formative years in a cloistered environment had left a gaping hole in my development. I was out of touch with the opportunities and demands of the secular world, and unprepared for normal adult responsibility. What would I do? Where would I live?

After the months that I had spent with my parents immediately after leaving Austin, I knew I could not live near them. My mother was so connected to me that she did not see me as a separate individual. All through my teens, she had unconsciously been forming me into her ideal mate. It never felt sexual, but I did not feel free to be myself. What she expected of me was unreal, and the person she wanted me to be was not who I knew myself to be.

I could sense that my father felt the undercurrent of my mother's attachment to me. My instinct told me that it got in the way of his relating to me as his son, and that he resented me for it. I remembered how, when I was still a lad, he would tell me that I should be more of a man. Perhaps he wanted me to be less timid. What neither he nor I understood was how much fear I had taken on from my mother. My parents did not have the self-knowledge to understand that the tension between them was directly affecting me. If their relationship was going through difficulty, then my security was threatened. I had long taken on the roles of mediator and peacemaker between them, and I would wrestle with this early conditioning for many years to come.

For most of my life, I had held an unchallenged belief that God was looking after me, and with the collapse of my trust in the Church, my sense of connection to God was shattered. That was even more disturbing than losing the Church. As the structures fell away, my belief in God was severely tested. The trauma of seeing the Church betray what I saw as a commitment to truth came as a terrible psychological blow. I had lost my former bearings and the foundation that I had relied on. I could no longer blindly trust that I was living under benign protection. During my first few years out in the world on my own, I would find it hard to feel any personal connections.

When I accepted that I could not live in New York, near my parents, the whole continent opened as an option. I needed to muster the courage to set off into the unknown. I knew that I would have to know my mind and go after what I wanted, but that was harder than I expected.

Setting out into the world made leaving the priesthood even more frightening to me. Not only was I going into the unknown, but the unknown was not assured to be working in my interest. I noticed that my feelings of disorientation were growing stronger, but I did not recognize that what I was experiencing was grief.

Somehow, my father saw what was happening and came to my assistance by asking me what I needed to take my next step. In the past, my mother would have intervened to see to my welfare, but she was too upset at the idea of my moving away to really see or help me. My father underwrote the cost of a new car, and established a bank account for me with several thousand dollars. He was actively helping me leave the priesthood and step into the life he had wanted for me. I never knew where my parents got the money came from, but they enabled me to begin the next part of my life.

After reviewing the places I had lived, I decided to return to British Columbia. I loved the interplay of the mountains and the sea there, along with the unspoiled natural environment, ancient trees, and easy access to some of the most beautiful places in the world, and those images drew me back.

Plus, the laity that I had met and worked with in Vancouver had progressive values that supported collaborative approaches to community; in fact, British Columbia was rich in the cultural heritage of First Nations. I was still known in some circles there, and I realized that I could call on people there to help me get settled. But I also realized that because they had known me as a priest, their response to me now, without that role, might be very different.

To my folks, British Columbia was on the other side of the world. They could already taste the loneliness they would experience with me living so far away. But they accepted my decision better than I expected. I planned to leave at the end of May—on the anniversary of my ordination, which had only been four years ago.

With the decision made about where to live, I began to make plans to travel. I had not spoken to Madeleine, or any of my friends, since I'd left, and now I called her in Texas, where she had moved to work at St. Austin, to bring her up to date. Hearing her on the phone, I realized how much we had supported each other during the four years we had worked together. There was so much to share. I started with my decision to leave the priesthood and head back to British Columbia. She told me that the pastor in St. Austin had dismantled the education program and terminated her job. The core group of lay people there had decided to keep together and do whatever they could to continue the work I had started. They had asked her to stay on in Austin and even found money for her salary. I knew that she had gone to Texas to work with me, and that her work there would not last long. I asked her if she would like to go back to British Columbia to work with me there. To my surprise, and delight, she agreed.

In my naivety, I did not clarify the level of emotional commitment that would be required to make a new life. I'd had very little experience with women. I did not even specify the nature of what I was asking her to do, or why she was coming with me. I only knew that I cared for her very deeply. We had worked collaboratively and closely. Our creative engagement had produced exciting programs and attracted people into a community. Ideas were the currency of our activity, and we both cherished our exciting working relationship.

But I had little experience with what was necessary to establish an emotional, romantic relationship. Being so inexperienced with emotional intimacy and sexually ignorant, I had no solid basis for establishing a happy relationship. When I arrived back in Austin, Madeleine agreed to tell people who were close to us in the parish that I was leaving the priesthood and that she had agreed to go away with me. The positive outpouring from the lay people was astounding. They all encouraged us and wished us well; in fact, they wondered why it had taken us so long to discover our attraction. I still had no picture what any of that meant. We simply packed up Madeleine's few belongings in a small cube trailer that we towed behind us as we headed to the Northwest.

Sex was really awkward. I had some experience of sex, but I had never established an ongoing relationship with anyone, except for my working friendship and professional partnership with Madeleine. Almost from the beginning of our association at the Catholic Center in Vancouver, we had shared a friendship based on our close, working partnership. Because I was a priest, our relationship naturally excluded romantic involvement; plus, physical intimacy would have compromised our ability to do our work. Talking was always easy, and I could feel passion about the ideas we discussed. But now I realized that after four years of suppressing any feelings of physical attraction, I could not look at Madeleine as a sexual partner without feeling twinges of guilt.

Unfortunately, we had no time to work through those feelings before setting off on a long car trip. Talking was still easy, but it did nothing to unleash passion. Madeleine had always thought of me as out of bounds romantically, and as we grew closer in other ways, she acknowledged that she did not feel any strong physical attraction toward me. In turn, I respected and even revered her, which further inhibited my sexual freedom. These complicated psychological issues didn't make it easy for us to come together.

As we drove West, we began to explore sexual intimacy. I enjoyed the euphoria of discovering each other in a new way. I was headed into a new life. I had a delightful companion and the sense that I was stepping into a free space, leaving my trials behind. I decided that we would work our our sexual issues over time. In the spirit of that hope, we made plans to get married as soon as I had a permanent job and paycheck.

Friends that Madeleine and I had known in Vancouver had moved to Vancouver Island, a three-hundred-mile-long island off the coast of southwest British Columbia, straddling the American boarder. My friend Harry was managing a moving company in Duncan, a community about forty miles north of Victoria, the capital of British Columbia, which sits on the southernmost end of Vancouver Island. Harry offered me a temporary job as a mover's assistant until I found a more permanent job.

The reality of the job market was as bad as I had feared. Everything was foreign to me. I found it impossible to write a resume that pointed to the value of my experience. Nonetheless, several interviews offered possibilities. I was offered a job as a textbook salesperson, but decided that I was ill-suited to that work. An Island school district was prepared to hire me as a counselor, but I lacked the teacher's certificate that was necessary for me to qualify.

A chance meeting with my friend Father Walter Donald, who had been a panelist with me on the "God Talk" radio show, opened the door to the nonprofit Family Services of Greater Victoria. Walter was a board member of the agency, and set up an interview for me with the executive director. The agency offered me a job, but the offer of employment was conditional on my becoming a registered social worker—another professional qualification I did not have. However, the universe was smiling on me. The government had only recently passed the *Social Worker Registration Act,* giving practitioners a year to register. In order to register, I would need a social work supervisor's letter attesting that I qualified. I traveled to Vancouver for an appointment with the head of the Catholic Family Services. His reception was a gift. He told me that from his experience of the counseling that I had done for his agency while I worked in Vancouver, I was fully qualified to be a registered social worker and gave me a letter to that effect. Now all I had to do was wait for the certificate to be issued, and I could begin working. When it arrived, I was given a starting date of August 15, 1969

On Sunday morning, July 21, astronaut Neil Armstrong opened the door of Apollo 11's lunar module the *Eagle,* and became the first human to step onto the surface of the moon. That night I stood on the front lawn of the home of my friend Harry and his wife Mary, looking to the sky. The moment seemed full of the possibilities that were opening to the human race. It was exhilarating watching the accomplishment of a feat that had been dreamed about over the entire history of humans on earth. The future looked bright. Madeleine and I had just rented a suite in an older home near the edge of Beacon Hill Park, and now we made plans to marry.

I got my first paycheck at the end of August. Madeleine and I took the hour-and-a-half ferry ride to Vancouver to get married, enjoying the beautiful Gulf Island scenery along the way. The Labor Day holiday offered us a three-day weekend. It took all the money I had to book a waterfront hotel room for our two-day honeymoon. We promised each other that we would make time for a more extended honeymoon as soon as we could afford it.

Although the shadow of the Church hung over our plans to marry, there was enough of the rebel in both Madeleine and me that we agreed to be married in the Church if we could arrange it. Because I was still technically a priest, and Madeleine had been divorced, neither of us was legally allowed to marry in the Catholic Church. But I got in touch with a priest friend in Vancouver who I knew could dispense with the legalities, and I was happy to discover that he was willing to bless our marriage vows. The vows we shared came from our hearts, and the love we experienced held the promise of a fulfilling life ahead.

The wedding party was small, with only Harry and Mary as witnesses. The priest who performed the wedding treated us to dinner at the top of Grouse Mountain, a ski lodge with magnificent views of both the city of Vancouver and Vancouver Island. On the table was a huge bouquet of roses sent by Pat and Will Barber, on behalf of all of our friends in Texas.

My first job presented an interesting challenge for me as an ex-priest. I was assigned to the unmarried-parents section of the agency. My role was to counsel women who were coping with an unwanted pregnancy. Listening to women pouring out their hearts about pregnancy was not new to me. I had heard confessions and counseled women about this situation as a priest. But now I was in a nonsectarian public agency. I could not impose religious standards on my clients. In the late 1960s, the prevailing choices were to keep the child or to place the child for adoption, and most of the women I counseled were distraught at the thought of putting their infant up for adoption.

Abortion was not a common choice for the women who came to the agency for counseling, but from time to time, there were women who wanted help in working through that choice. Any judgments I had held in the past about the morality of terminating a pregnancy were eclipsed by observing the deeply human struggle that these women were going through. No one took the decision lightly, and almost all of the women I spoke with weighed the life of the fetus in the balance of their decision-making.

Inevitably, after a gut-wrenching counseling session with an anguished client, I would come away feeling as if I had just been in the confessional. I never attempted to confer absolution in the formal sense, but I was always conscious of that parallel, and I did whatever I could to lift the burden from the shoulders of the mother-to-be.

The agency had an adoption department that screened prospective adopting parents, and arranged for a placement after birth. After one deeply moving session, I shared with Madeleine, within the limits of confidentiality, how moved I was by the suffering of one of my clients. Madeleine confided to me something she had never previously told me: She had given birth to a child who was placed for adoption. For a young woman of Italian Catholic culture, who had had no understanding or support from her family, the experience had been akin to exile, leaving her feeling ashamed and psychologically scarred. It certainly had affected her experience of sex, and now her sharing her story with me shed some light on our private struggle.

I decided that what I needed was to be a member of a church, and began visiting each of the parishes in Victoria to see where I best fit. I assumed that Bishop Remi De Roo, had been a member of the majority reform group at the Vatican Council, would have imprinted the spirit of the Council on the parishes in his diocese. He had spoken and written eloquently about the reforms Vatican II had proposed. But there was little evidence of a Vatican II renewal in any of the parishes I attended, including the cathedral. I frustrated to the point of anger. The way the priests celebrated the Eucharist and the quality of their preaching did not reflect the theology that the Council had taught, nor did it show any awareness of there having been a movement toward a major reform of the Church.

Every Sunday, I would sit in the pew and seethe at what I was hearing from the pulpit. Negative attitudes toward people and an archaic understanding of theology left me feeling like it might be better not to be there at all. After several months of this experience, I decided that I was simply wrong to go to Mass to get angry, so I stopped going. Madeleine gave up before I did.

As we settled into life in Victoria, I found myself growing progressively sadder. In retrospect, I realize that I was grieving all the losses I had recently experienced. Madeleine was also experiencing a loss of identity, community, and prominence within the Church. We were each feeling more withdrawn, and we found it difficult to remember the dynamic contribution we had once made to people's lives.

For me, I had lost the Paulist community, the priesthood, and the identity I had been forging since I entered the seminary fourteen years before. But what made all those losses more acute was my loss of faith and membership in the Church. That last loss came gradually, but hit harder than all the others. Having witnessed the Pope's cynical denial of the truth so obvious to me, I could no any longer believe anything the Church stood for. What had once been the center of my life was simply turning to sand.

o o o

A low-level depression overtook my psyche. I could no longer savor the ordinary pleasures of life. I imagined I was in an empty vat, with no light coming from anywhere. I told myself that I simply had to ride over the top of the emptiness and get on with living. Nonetheless, the depression would not leave me.

In the void created by the disappearance of my faith, I began to wonder if all the religions that spoke about spirit and spirituality were in touch with some reality that could be discovered outside the realm of dogma. Was there a basis for a conviction that the world was more than material? According to science, the only reality is that which can be measured or weighed. But was that really so? I did not believe it, but I had no evidence of Spirit in the universe. I began to read and explore other cosmological possibilities.

My distress began settling into my body as well as my psyche. I resolved to exercise to overcome the stiffness, and recruited a handball partner. But while playing one evening after work, I felt a twist in my back and the beginning of intense pain. I saw my doctor right away, and was instructed to stop playing handball and adopt a lighter exercise regime. After a few weeks of no relief, as I was getting out of bed one morning, I twisted to avoid stepping on my dog, who slept on the floor next to the bed, and fell suddenly to the floor in excruciating pain. I could not move and was taken to the hospital in an ambulance. X-rays were taken and a spinal tap performed to determine the extent of the damage. I had ruptured a disc in the lumbar region.

Dr. Fouad Hamdi, the specialist who took my case, was a visiting surgeon from Egypt who was doing cutting-edge surgery with artificial vertebras. He had developed a procedure that repaired the disc, but did not require the back to be fused or pinned. When he described the procedure to me, I was impressed by his confidence. I wanted to recover the full use of my back that he promised. When I asked him what would happen if he made a mistake, he looked at me for some time and then said, "My good man, I don't make mistakes."

After surgery, as I was coming out of the anesthetic in the recovery room, I had a vision of a V shape above the point of the pain. In the V were the faces of clients, union colleagues, and many other people in my life who were making demands of me. It was clear that the rupture of the disc was related to the pressure I had put myself under, and this vision gave me a new appreciation for the connection between the inner and outer worlds.

I had only been out of the hospital for a short while when my mother called to tell me that my father was dying. She did not think that he had much more time. I told her that Madeleine and I would be there right away as long as the doctor said I could fly. A few days later, we were in my dad's room in Southampton Hospital. He was under a plastic tent with oxygen tubes helping him breathe, and when he saw me, he signaled to me to open the plastic flap, so I did. Each breath was a struggle, and speaking was very difficult for him. He beckoned me to come closer to him, and when I did, he reached up, put his arms around my neck, and hugged me for the longest time. He brought his lips near to my ear, and whispered, "I love you." He had not said those words to me since I had become a teenager. Tears streamed down my face as I told him that I loved him with all my heart.

At one point, when Madeleine and I were alone with my dad, something happened that she could not believe. I had bent forward over my dad in his bed, taking a position that she later told me she was sure must have been very painful for me so soon after surgery. But I had been completely unaware of myself, and could only experience my closeness to my father. I stayed with him for several hours that day, mostly in silent communion. When the staff told us it was time to go home, I told my dad that I would see him the next day, but he died in the small hours of the morning.

Madeleine and I stayed on with my mother and helped her through the funeral Mass at the parish church in Southampton. My mother was devastated. She had been caring for Dad for several years, and he had been the sole focus of her days. Now she was arranging to bury the man who was her life partner for almost forty years. She also wanted to have a funeral service at Our Lady of Lourdes, the family parish in Queens Village, where my parents had spent most of their lives. I had said my first Mass as a priest in that church. Madeleine and I accompanied my mother to both Masses. At each service, old friends consoled her, and depending on how close they were, she sometimes broke down and let her tears flow.

We accompanied my father's body to the cemetery in Queens Village, where he was buried next to my grandfather and grandmother and three of Mom's brothers. I was shocked to see that my mother had chiseled both my father's and her names on the granite stone. There was a place reserved for her beside him. I invited her to come stay with us in Victoria, but she declined outright. Despite all the time Madeleine had spent together with my parents while Dad was still alive, whether at our home in Victoria or theirs in Southampton, my mother harbored a strong resentment of Madeleine. The way she saw it, Madeleine had lured me from the priesthood. Their relationship was formal and testy. I knew Mom would never want to come live with us, but I still hated the idea of leaving her alone in such a vulnerable state. Nonetheless, my time off work was limited, and eventually Madeleine and I had to leave.

My father's death deeply affected me. Even though he had chronic emphysema, I had not been prepared for him to die at what seemed an early age. I had been deeply touched by his giving voice to his love for me, and the depth of his feelings made his passing even more poignant. I needed help to go through grieving again. I was holding a lot inside, and keeping up a brave front, but in the end, I could not do it. I was not coping well at work or at home. I had become the supervisor of a social work team responsible for the protection of abused and neglected children, and my recollections of the angry verbal abuse I had received from my father was complicating the mix of feelings that I had to sort through on a daily basis.

My friend Graham Miles, a psychiatrist who had worked with me to help many disturbed children on our caseload, was a kind and helpful counselor for me. It was the first time that I would seek psychiatric help, and I did not realize how much it could help. I was acutely aware that with my father's death, my principal anchor in the world was gone. I felt like an orphan. As long as my father was alive, I had felt I had a foundation. But with him gone, I felt I had lost my footing. As a priest ministering to grieving parishioners, I had seen the comfort that belief in heaven and eternal life can bring, and now, I had lost that belief. I did not have any way of believing in the teachings of the Church, now that I had seen it be so false.

Gradually, I came to accept that I was now the adult in the way I had reserved for my father. I needed to be a man who could stand on his own feet. I grew up in my acceptance of myself, but I longed all the more for spiritual reassurance. I knew that the Church could no longer provide that for me, and I had not yet discovered a basis for spirituality apart from the Church.

A few years after my father died, my mother surprised me by announcing that she wanted to visit Madeleine and me in Victoria for a few weeks. She proposed bringing her friend Ellen, who had taught school with her when they were both young. I wasn't sure how we would manage that visit since Madeleine and I were both working, and so far, nothing had occurred to thaw the tension between my mom and my wife.

Nevertheless, I was happy that my mother had relented enough to visit us. She and Ellen wanted to see the World's Fair in Spokane, Washington, so I took a few days off to drive them there. The trip through through the Cascade Mountains to eastern Washington was a beautiful drive, and I thought they would enjoy the trip.

But while I was driving, I had the most unnerving experience. My mother and her friend were sitting in the back seat of my car, deeply engaged in conversation with each other. Listening to them talking, I suddenly found myself growing more and more angry until I was in a seething rage. As far as I could tell, there was nothing in the content of their conversation to provoke such angry feelings. I kept the feeling within and did not speak or reveal how angry I was. I tried to figure out what had triggered my rage, but was unable to identify it. And yet, my feelings were so intense, I thought I was going mad.

During the rest of the visit, the experience did not recur, but my concern about my sanity remained. As soon as my mother and Ellen returned to New York, I resolved to address the experience. My search for an intervention brought me to a public presentation in Victoria by Dr. Ben Wong, a well-known child psychiatrist in Vancouver, and Dr. Jock McKeen, a medical doctor with a specialty in Chinese medicine, who were doing ground-breaking work together in group therapy. At the end of the talk, when they announced the workshop they would conduct that weekend, I signed up immediately.

Dr. McKeen and Dr. Wong were holding the workshop at the university, and I arrived to find about twenty people, mostly women, in the room. Their work was body-centered, and they were able to identify blocked areas in the flow of energy, or Chi. They released the blocks by having the participants who volunteered as subjects do very deep breathing, and then applying physical pressure or doing acupuncture. The participants each experienced such an intense release of physical and emotional energy that it terrified me, and I held back from volunteering. I did, however, stiffen my resolve and signed up for the weeklong "Come Alive" workshop, which was to be held at Cold Mountain on Cortes Island, north of Victoria, between Vancouver Island and the mainland.

Close to forty men and women attended the "Come Alive" workshop at Cold Mountain. Dr. Wong and Dr. McKeen began by arranging us in a large circle. They already knew many of the participants who had been their patients in Vancouver. The bodywork began right away, with the first volunteer lying on a mat in the center of the circle and the two doctors and their assistant standing over his body, scanning for blocks. When the lease process began, it was accompanied by a horrific release of anguish, followed by intense sobbing. Once the man's emotions were spent, he talked about the experience with Dr. Wong, who tenderly embraced him. The two doctors then asked the circle to gather around the man and hold him in a collective embrace. I was enthralled, and could not shift my eyes away for a second. I felt like I was observing a healing that was akin to an exorcism, except that it was entirely without any religious overtones.

The doctors worked on at least two participants each morning, afternoon, and evening session. Sometimes the emotions of the volunteer in the center of the circle touched a chord in me, so that my reciprocal emotion was released automatically.

I was holding back, as I often did in my life, afraid to step forward. As I sat observing other people's experiences, one man's work deeply touched me and I began crying quietly. One of the assistants asked me if I was ready to do my own work, and I agreed. I stepped forward and lay down on the mattress at the center of the circle, and began to breathe deeply. The leaders encouraged me to imagine filling my body completely with my breath. My body began to vibrate and warmth spread out into my limbs, hands, and feet. I watched as Dr. Wong and Dr. McKeen ran their hands up and down, a few inches from my body, sensing any areas where there was a temperature or energy change, and conferring with each other as they worked. Finally, they began to apply pressure on my legs, working deep into the large muscles, and I screamed with pain.

Suddenly I was flooded with excruciating feelings of abandonment and sadness. The intensity was stronger than any emotion I had ever previously experienced. In the midst of the rush of emotion, I had a visual memory: I saw myself walking behind the legs of a woman dressed in a skirt, stockings, and high heels. She went out a door that closed in my face.

As I allowed myself to fully experience my feelings, I felt a sense of release and elation. It was as if I were bouncing off the ceiling. As the work concluded, the group gathered around me, lifted me into a cradle made by their joined hands and arms, and rocked me gently. In the background, soothing music played. I felt comforted, cared for, and ecstatic.

That week, I also managed to get in touch with the intensity of my stored-up anger a few times. My anger was related to my sense of abandonment, and the intensity of its power scared me. Each time I encountered it, I was helped to release it safely, with no one being alarmed by what I was releasing.

After the workshop, I called my mother and asked her if my memory rang a bell with her. She told me that she keenly recalled a time when I was about two and she was going back to teaching. She had hired a caregiver to look after me, and every day, when I became upset at her going, she felt distressed about having to leave me.

I figured out that I experienced that event as being abandoned. The feelings were too intense for a two-year-old and instead of being experienced, they had lodged in my musculature. When I got in touch with those emotions through the circle work, it came back as a current experience which had major ramifications. Any time I sensed any hint of being left out or not included, the present-time experience echoed into the past and magnified it so that the event of my mother leaving me had greater than appropriate significance.

I began to see the importance of my inner experiences. I discussed the circle work process and my insights with Madeleine, who told me that it seemed to shed light on aspects of my personality that she had previously observed. My new awareness of how much my inner experience was colored by how I saw the outer world, and visa versa, made me realize that I needed to do more inner work. My Cold Mountain work had begun a new phase of life for me. I did several more workshops dealing with anger I had never admitted or expressed, and discovered that I had repressed anger toward both my parents, though it was more complicated with my mother. When I was a child, I was never allowed to express angry feelings; whenever I was angry with my mother, I could only keep it inside. Expressing taboo feelings with others who had undergone similar experiences as my witnesses made the release of anger easier for me. I was relieved to find that I was not the only person who went through such feelings.

I also spent a week dealing with sex and identity. I had repressed my sexual feelings for years, and it was playing havoc with me now. My discovery of the reason behind my awkwardness with women really helped me gain some freedom in my relationship with Madeleine, and subsequently, with lovers.

Around that time, I also became interested in Transcendental Meditation, after hearing the well-known musician Paul Horn talk about his own TM experiences and reading about the Beatles discovering Maharishi Mahesh Yogi, TM's founder. Paul Horn extolled the value of stilling the mind and finding a core of peace within, and I was entranced by the idea. I decided to learn to meditate. There was a TM center in Victoria, and I joined a class for beginners. The instructor gave me basic lessons on how to deal with the incessant thoughts that came into my mind, and how to go into the silence of a quiet mind. I was given a mantra, a Sanskrit word that did not have a translation. Repeating the word allows the mind to focus, which helps in the quieting process. I adopted the practice of meditating every morning and evening, allowing my mind to quiet down and to seek out the source of all potential.

In the years to come, my meditation practice did wonders to keep me calm and centered, reuce my stress level, and enable me to concentrate more clearly. Recognizing that the voice in my head had nothing to do with reality, I began to realize the extent to which I was co-creating my reality. I came to understand how much was going on in my mind that was just the product of my thoughts; at the same time, my thoughts have the power to create what I interpret as reality. This awareness gave me much more of a sense of responsibility for my thoughts.

My religious foundation was beginning to crack away. Although I had abandoned the religion I'd grown up with, it was still governing my thinking. The constraints of my belief system had all been adopted, so that they became my own. They had come in from the outside, and I had not chosen them. I was not my beliefs. I was not my religion or my morality. I had choice. I was responsible for my behavior. the code of religion provided neither right nor wrong. I did not have to uphold the code, nor did I have to reject it. I felt an enormous sense of inner freedom. I had not yet found a new spirituality, but I had begun the process of looking in the right direction.

My insights made me more aware of my inner impulses. I began entertaining the view that there is no objective right or wrong. The idea of a divine law giver is bound up with the Judeo/Christian mind. It was also one side of the debate in the early Catholic Church between those who adopted the approach that morality was found in the following of rules, and those who followed the approach attributed to Jesus in the Gospels, that the whole of the law is contained in the idea of love: Love God and your fellow humans. However, I was not approaching any of this in an academic sense. I wanted to free myself from all vestiges of superstition that I had simply accepted as a package. What was good for me? How should I act toward others, and why? Those were my real questions.

In the 1970s, my work involved a lot of family counseling. My heart was often touched by the pain I contacted in the people who came to see me. I was often attracted to the women I counseled and believed that I could help them. There was, at times, a strong current of sexual drive. One of my clients was a single parent who was unable to manage one of her two children, and the ministry had taken the child into care. The mother developed a strong attraction to me, and I found her very desirable. From the outset, I knew that it would be unethical for me to become intimate with her, because of the power relationship that existed with me having control over the life of her child. But that rational awareness did nothing to minimize the strength of the attraction for me. I usually limited my contact with my clients to the office, and I kept the door open and always had someone else in the vicinity as a safeguard.

But on one occasion, the after-hours duty worker contacted me to deal with one of the woman's children, who had been picked up by the police. The duty worker asked me to bring the child home to her mother. The mother was upset by the child's behavior, so rather than making an office appointment at a later time, I accepted her invitation to come to her house for a cup of coffee so we could talk at once. The sexual energy between us became evident before very long. It was all I could do not to succumb to my overwhelming urges. I wanted her and it was clear she wanted me. I almost wound up bolting from the house. An observer might have laughed at the scene, but to me it was unnerving and embarrassing. I had to transfer the child to another worker to avoid the necessity of continuing contact with the mother. She began to call me at home, to send me presents, to invite me to come to her church with her. I had not talked with Madeleine about the experience, which further complicated the dynamic. I felt trapped.

There was no questioning the power of the attraction, and I realized that it could easily have led me into an obsession. I was torn between my desire and my need for self-preservation. My own urges and attraction made the situation explosive, but I realized that if I crossed the invisible line, my career could be terminated. In the end, the circumstances and my sense of self-preservation restrained me. The woman knew that I was married, but that was not enough to make any difference. I did not feel noble, and I was certainly not in charge of the situation. Finally, in order to establish a safe boundary, I had to be firm to the point of rudeness. I wound up rejecting her, which was the last thing I really wanted.

As the decade came to a close, and I more consciously weighed whether to adhere to the moral code that had been part of my Catholic upbringing, I entertained the possibility of doing otherwise. In the incident with the woman who was my client, the power of the sexual allure was intensified by the lack of conscious freedom of choice. Because I believed that I did not have a choice, the erotic became hypercharged. The experience also awakened in me an awareness of the absence of a satisfying sex life at home. I could rationalize that my marriage was based on friendship, not sex, which was true. But I was not acknowledging the fact that sex was missing. Madeleine was my soul mate, but while much of the relationship was satisfying, my sexual urges were growing stronger. My self-image as someone in control of my passions constrained my behavior. But feelings that are not acknowledged have a way of growing stronger and blowing up in ways that are unexpected.

I had become a supervisor of a social service office with twenty staff members reporting to me. We were responsible for child welfare service and income assistance. The office also did community development work in the area, and was running a successful program of parent education and preventative intervention. I reached out in love and tenderness to one of the staff members, a single mother with one child at home. Again, I found myself limiting my freedom, contending with the rule that it was inappropriate to become intimate with a subordinate. To betray my wife was wrong in my value system, and it was wrong to enter an affair that could injure a number of people. I understand that, but it did not constrain my behavior.

The emptiness I was feeling, the loss of my spiritual compass, and my underdeveloped sexual maturity all conspired to blind me for quite a while. When I told Madeleine that I was going to leave her, I was pierced by the hurt in her eyes. I could feel in one brief moment the pain I was causing, and that was stronger and more compelling than any rationalization I could make in my mind. I realized that I could not enter another relationship unless I had come to terms with the relationship I had with Madeleine. At the same time, the pull toward the lovely and sensitive young woman who worked for me was overpowering. I wanted nothing more than to be with her. Everything about her called to me.

When I reflect on the power of my mind to create my world, nothing could be clearer: I chose to be attracted to a person I knew I was not free to pursue. I was married, she was my employee, and we were constrained by ethical as well as professional rules. I was being recklessly rebellious, and ignoring my conscience.

In the end I did not go through with the affair, and there was pain as well as learning in that. Both Madeleine and the other woman suffered from my behavior. I was acting in self-induced blindness that could have been even more destructive than it turned out. I knew I needed to find a way to be sexual without being hurtful of others. It would need a major adjustment in my relationship with Madeleine and I would have to be more careful about who I became involved with.

Eventually, Madeleine and I did find a compromise, but not for quite a while. In the meantime, I realized that I was still in a relationship with Madeleine, and that I wanted to honor that. I despised myself for not being straight and open. I would never again hurt her the way I had. I did not really want a separation, but rather a way to honor my wife without sacrificing myself. We did find a way to do more than compromise. It would come in the context of my aspiration to become a leader at a higher level than a social work supervisor. I had the opportunity to run for president of a large provincial union with its headquarters in a different city than the one in which Madeleine and I lived. I had stumbled badly in the darkness of my own inner landscape. Now I was on my way to freedom, although it would take a while for me to reach it.

$$\left(\,4\,\right)$$

An Unusual Spiritual Path

*A hero ventures forth from the world of common day into
a region of supernatural wonder: fabulous forces are there
encountered and a decisive victory is won: the hero comes
back from this mysterious adventure with the power to
bestow boons on his fellow man.*[1]

—Joseph Campbell

FOR THE NEXT twenty-five years of my life, I walked a path
that few would consider part of a spiritual journey. First I was
a union activist and then I was elected as the head of the British
Columbia Government Service Employees Union (BCGEU). For
me, this experience brought me my greatest learning, as well as my
toughest challenges.

When I started out in social work, within the public service

---

[1] Joseph Campbell. *The Hero with a Thousand Faces.* Novato, California: New
World Library, 2008, p. 23. In *The Hero with a Thousand Faces,* Joseph Campbell
described a pattern that each of us follows in our personal journey. Campbell's
template is useful in understanding my struggle to capture of the grail, recover
a sense of personal spirituality, and to bring benefit to the people I served. The
mythic hero's journey is my metaphor.

of British Columbia, I never thought of it as a hero's journey. My experience as a family counselor, child protection social worker, and team leader in the Ministry of Social Services engaged me with helping others. For a while, I was the supervisor of Victoria Day Care Information Services. Day-to-day work in the field of abused and neglected children in the city's core neighborhood exposed me to the underlying problems faced by so many troubled families.

The effects of poverty bedeviled many families I met. Often, the problems that brought my clients to me stemmed from the lack of adequate finances. The pressure on single-wage families, whether headed by one parent or two, often manifested in the abusive treatment of the children. I felt like I was working at the discharge end of the social injustice pipe, and the solutions were higher in the social system.

While I was serving as a family and child protection social worker, I also volunteered as a union activist. When the government took over the agency where I worked, I was the head of an independent union representing all of the workers. The government had a legal obligation to honor the employees' existing contract, even though it had not extended bargaining rights to them. I had a representational role, negotiating for social service workers in the first round of bargaining between the BCGEU and the New Democratic Party government.

A few years later, the Social Credit Party returned to power. Despite its different ideological bent, the new government continued to negotiate productively with the union. However, in the late 1970s and early '80s, inflation ran wild and the federal government introduced wage and price controls. The officials at the bargaining table displayed a very different attitude as the government began a ten-year assault against the labor movement, especially the union that represented its own employees.

Throughout that time, I held most of the volunteer executive positions in the union, and I became convinced that the union would have to strengthen the role of its representatives in the workplace. All of the power and authority were concentrated in the headquarters operation, whose representatives showed up when the union needed to rely on the local leadership to conduct a province-wide strike. I advocated that the union become more democratic, and that elected volunteers like me needed to take more responsibility.

Within the executive, I became an outspoken advocate for changing the constitution of the union to make the leadership more accountable to the membership. I became impatient with autocratic decision-making. The union needed the checks and balances that only strong elected leadership provides.

My buried resentment at the Pope's autocratic behavior reared its head as I honed in on people in authority who were behaving badly. Righting the power balance to give more say to the membership became the theme of all of my reforms in the union.

Over the course of my many years as a union leader, I mined nuggets of self-knowledge from the inner depths of my subconscious. The learning was slow and sometimes painful, but at the heart of what I learned was the spiritual lesson that there is no distinction between the outer world and the inner one.

After going through several rounds of bargaining that ended in strikes, I came to my first significant realization about myself: I had compulsive behavior patterns to which I had been blind. What better occupation could I have chosen in order to repeatedly and legitimately challenge authority? The government was the ultimate authority. As the employer, it was the immovable object attracting the irresistible force of the employees' representative. As the head of the union, with a mandate from the members to make gains on their behalf, I repeatedly went into battle as the hero. I relished this role.

As a child, I had struggled with my father over his misuse of authority. In my fifties, I came to realize that every few years, as a union leader, I was repeatedly reenacting my power struggle with my father. Bargaining a large collective agreement that covers thirty-five thousand people is a major undertaking. It requires extensive preparation, a great deal of ritual in the bargaining process, and many pieces that are important in themselves. But I did not make the connection between my union work and the psychological work until I had an awakening.

Four years after becoming president of the union, I went through an experience that resulted in an explosive crisis that almost cost me my job. It was a clash o ideologies and power agendas at the highest political level in my province, and its impact resonated in my very core.

A few months after Bill Vander Zalm was elected as Premier of British Columbia, he invited me to a meeting that would determine both of our fates. At the meeting, he announced that he planned to change the public sector into a profit-driven private-sector moneymaker. He had an elaborate scheme worked out. The government would offload huge sections of the public service and then healthcare and education to the private sector. He foresaw making huge financial gains in the process. The public service—the members of my union—would be the first to go. The Premier's principal secretary told my executive, "The only thing that will stop us is political expediency."

I came out of the meeting stunned. I thought to myself "I am going to be the last president of the BCGEU. There will be no public service and no union left when he is through." I believe I said aloud to my colleagues, that we were the only ones who could possibly stop the Premier's plan.

This was in the era dominated by the privatization agendas of Prime Minister Margaret Thatcher in Great Britain, President Ronald Reagan in the United States, and Prime Minister Brian Mulroney in Canada, so the ideology behind Premier Vander Zalm's grandiose scheme was familiar to me. I resolved to oppose his plan as forcefully as I could.

Philosophically, I believe in the public good. I believe passionately that many things, especially healthcare and protection of the environment, should not be left to the profit motive. To me, the elimination of the public service in government was madness, and I told the Premier that I would oppose him.

For the next nine months, I mounted a campaign to protect public services. I traveled to every city and major community in British Columbia, a territory the size of Washington, Oregon, and California combined. In each community, I met with the local Labor Council and Chamber of Commerce, along with the municipal leaders. I showed business leaders the amount of money that flowed into the local economy from the public service payroll, and what was at stake from the loss of well-paid government jobs.

I generated media coverage everywhere I went, and letters of opposition began flooding the Premier's office. Editorials in local and provincial papers began questioning the objective of privatizing the whole public sector. People valued public healthcare and public education. They wanted their roads plowed on a winter night by government employees, and they wanted children and the environment protected from abuse.

I could tell I was being effective. Criticism started coming from Social Credit supporters. The government's public relations machine called me a special interest group, and said that I was opposing the plans of a legitimately elected government. Over the course of that year, a great deal of public attention was paid to the contest between the union and the government.

The province-wide campaign ended as we were scheduled to begin collective bargaining. The talks covered normal bargaining issues, but the major focus was on the privatization package. When the negotiations bogged down over the union's right to thwart the will of the government, I had to admit that, as a citizen, I had no right to stop them, and that I could only make the cost of doing what they wanted prohibitive. We went on strike to drive home our point, and received a surprising level of support from the public. Editorials pointed out that we were trying to protect the services that people were now complaining were not available to them because of the strike.

The bargaining sessions were intense, with feelings running high on both sides. I was so intent on winning the day that when the mediator told me that our vice president was hampering our discussions because of his behavior, instead of taking him aside and coaching him to act differently, I simply excluded him from the final hours of discussion.

When a settlement finally was reached, I felt triumphant, and brought the settlement to the bargaining committee. To my utter surprise, they seemed downcast and disgruntled, and only offered half-hearted congratulations. I could not understand their tepid response after such a long struggle to stop the ravages of full-scale privatization. I could tell that the man I had excluded from the table had been working on the bargaining committee members out of his hurt feelings. When I finally asked the committee what was wrong, one of the women I trusted to be straight with me told me that they were disappointed with me. I had left them out, and turned the negotiation into a one-person show. It was all about me. Because I was acting very differently from the way they knew me, they did not feel any ownership of the outcome. If the outcome was less than perfect, they did not feel it was their job to sell it to their members.

The membership of the union, on the other hand, voted overwhelmingly to approve the new contract, seeing the benefit it brought them. Unfortunately, I was not able to undo one of the privatizations that had already been pushed through. The Ministry of Transportation's Road and Bridge Maintenance crews had been handed over to individual contractors. The highways employees mostly followed their work over to their new employers. Nonetheless, there was unhappiness among the crews, because we had promised we would do everything to keep them employed in government.

At the union's convention, which was scheduled within a few months after the contract was ratified, I expected the members to be upbeat, sharing in the success of thwarting privatization of their work, but instead, there was an agitated mood. I had proposed a reorganization of the internal representational structure, in order to accommodate the growth we were experiencing from organizing new members. Some of the executive would lose their positions, which further fueled their discontent.

When the time came to elect new officers, the mood had turned sour. Two members of the bargaining committee, including the one I had offended, announced that they would be running against me. I had not been challenged since first becoming president. I was stunned not to be ahead on the first ballot. On the third ballot, I barely squeaked by, winning by only twelve votes.

After the convention, I was despondent. I had poured my heart and energy into the campaign to frustrate the government agenda and succeeded. Yet there did not seem to be any gratitude from the members. Even though I had won the election and would serve another term, I felt defeated.

I retreated to my Gulf Island cabin. For more than a week, I nursed my wounds and bordered on depression. Madeleine counseled me to be aware of my dreams, certain that I would receive guidance from my subconscious. That night I did have a vivid dream. My grandmother appeared to me as though she were in the room, telling me to pay attention to my heroes.

When I awoke, I told Madeleine about the dream and began to

make a list of all the people I regarded as heroes: John and Bobby Kennedy, Martin Luther King, Tommy Douglas, and David Suzuki were at the top of the list. By the time I had completed my roster, there was no *zing* of recognition of how any of them related to my grandmother's advice.

How did my grandmother's advice, to be aware of my heroes, resolve my dilemma? Perhaps there were other heroes I had not considered. Radio had been the storyteller of my boyhood. Shows like *Superman*, *Tom Mix*, and *The Lone Ranger* aired regularly. As soon as the Lone Ranger came to mind, I knew I had struck gold. I recognized immediately that I was acting like him. He was the hero in the white hat who rode into town on his horse Silver to rescue people from some dreadful crisis. He was strong and noble and always protected the underdog; in the final scene of each show, he would ride out of town to the grateful thanks of the crowd.

This was my myth: I was the lone hero. I saw in myself the hero in every story from *The Odyssey* to *Star Wars*. I had incorporated the lone hero archetype as my own; in fact, the lone hero had been my personal myth since boyhood. Once I had been triggered by hearing the premier's plan, everything I heard was interpreted through that myth. I was the actor, but it was the myth telling the story.

This insight hit me like a thunderclap. I had taken a mythic view, with myself as the hero, even before I went to school. Every time I was challenged, I would go into lone-hero mode. As I reviewed my life, I realized how many times that myth had been at play—from my clashes with my father to tackling a provincial premiery.

How could this myth have been so influential without me realizing that it was working in me? Because I was on vacation, I had the leisure to contemplate my discovery. I realized that the lone hero myth had given me a story that enabled me to face the crises in my life. Whenever I was challenged, the myth came alive within me and ran on its own to the end of every story. The story I believed about myself was sitting in my subconscious, ready to become an action template.

My myth perpetuated my early sense of isolation and separation. As a template, it gave me clues about how to act nobly in the face of any challenge. The lone hero needed no help to face the dragon. When it was operative, there was no place in my story for helpmates.

As I examined all the implications of the Lone Ranger's influence, I wondered whether I was stuck with that story for life. Clearly, it was not working in my present circumstances. I had internalized the story unconsciously, so could I consciously change it? I began to review other heroic myths to see if any of them fit. Each time a mythic hero occurred to me, I wrote down his name along with everything that I knew about that particular figure. Then I compared that story to the circumstances and values that I now found in my life.

Two figures from mythology emerged repeatedly: Merlyn, the wizard, who was the teacher and mentor of Arthur, who would become king. I liked Merlyn's wisdom. He contributed to the world by training the future king. Yet, despite its appeal, that image did not fully fit me. Merlyn was a loner, and I'd had enough of being one.

I was most attracted to King Arthur when he was older, presiding over the roundtable. He governed with compassion and wisdom, and inspired his knights to deeds of valor, commissioning the bravest of them to seek the Holy Grail. This was to become my new myth. I thought about Arthur, dreamed about him, wrote down the things I liked about him, and then put that myth away.

When I returned to work, I acted differently. I made more considered decisions, and I found that those around me reacted to me differently as well. Things went smoothly. Discussions with senior advisors produced solid and effective plans. I seemed to be in a new flow, with fewer struggles and greater effectiveness.

As the days unfolded, I realized that what I was doing was not about me. I had simply shifted to make others the center of my motivation. I was the leader of a large organization, and my executives were all representatives of the membership. We had a collective role to play in protecting the members and promoting their interests. This was no different from what it had been before, but now I was seeing it differently.

For the next ten years, I was a different person: strong without being overbearing, and able to be straight without worrying about what people would think about me. I accepted challenges without cringing, and if someone else was right, I more readily admitted it and incorporated their viewpoint. I began to grow wiser. Perhaps the wisdom of Merlyn as well as the nobility of Arthur were in me. My new myth fit my situation, and was a good inspiration.

Why did I accept the challenge of heading the union? At the time, I was very reluctant to become president. It required me to give up my job as a social worker helping troubled families, a pastoral role that was familiar to me, and immerse myself entirely in the field of labor relations. Moreover, I became responsible for a large, complex organization with about thirty-six thousand members.

The union was a large entity as well, with approximately forty staff representatives and an equal number of administrative personnel, and there were two unions representing those staff members. I was responsible for a multimillion-dollar budget.

Most troubling to me, I did not see myself reflected among the other union leaders of the time. Although I had been on the executive for ten years by then, I did not consider myself a professional labor relations practitioner. I still saw myself as a volunteer, a well-informed amateur, not a tough labor union head.

I was reluctant to take on a high-profile position that would require stepping into the archetype of the warrior. I had avoided the need to exercise my inner warrior. I preferred the quieter, gentler, voice-of-reason persona. To become the union's leader, I would need to have the warrior's courage and strength.

But I wanted to make a real difference in the world, so I stepped up to the challenge of becoming president. My formative experience with Father Daniel Berrigan still remained with me and shaped my motivation.

I spent another ten years as president after my moment of enlightenment, and decided to use the power of my office to affect change. I would lead the union through deep transformational growth. I recognized the opportunity not only to change my own union but also have an impact on the broader labor movement. But I knew that I needed to be clear about my motives as well as have a clear moral compass to guide me in turbulent times.

I wanted to help my fellow workers, and to do something for the marginalized people in the workplace. Remembering the parents I had dealt with as a social worker, I wanted to give more money and opportunity to these workers for their families. During my first four years of navigating the waters of high-stakes power politics, I had developed the confidence to be myself and not feel embarrassed by the fact that I needed to be powerful on behalf of others.

"Give priority to the needs of the poor." This was one concept that I had retained from Vatican II, and in the workplace of the 1990s, women were the poor. They were paid less than men doing the same work. That glaring statistic fired my indignation. Most women worked for wages that fell below the poverty line, and older women lived in poverty because, based on their employment years, they had less access to pensions. I found that appalling. I was in a position to change that.

I persuaded the union to make a major shift and reach out to the unorganized. At that time, most male government employees were relatively secure, and reasonably well paid. But not the women. All around us, the women workers were poor, second-class citizens who needed what the union could provide.

I asked the union to adopt organizing as a key mode of work. We would restructure the budget to put more resources into outreach to the women who worked in credit unions and banks, social services, and healthcare—all of whom were all underpaid, compared to the males in the public sector.

At the same time, women in the public service could not claim equal pay for work of equal value to men. I was able to persuade the first woman premier and her minister responsible for women's issues to negotiate a framework with the union to bring about pay equity for women in the provincial public service. We agreed that this would be outside of normal bargaining, and would not affect our collective agreement.

I gave one of my staff members, an expert in the classifications, the mandate to work with the government to achieve a gender-neutral classification system. Although it took us several years to complete, we attained pay equity. That accomplishment had enormous effects and was one of my greatest achievements. I also made a commitment to help the newly organized bargaining units to improve the lot of families, seeing that as a spiritual decision, putting resources to work to end poverty wherever I could.

During my years as president, I grew more confident, drawing strength as I faced each successive challenge. I began to align my inner world with my outer one, knowing that integrity must be based on honest and trustworthy dealings with everyone. I brought my inner integrity into all of my public actions, and my reputation became my most valued asset.

I began to see the integration of my inner and outer lives as a spiritual value. The spiritual wisdom that emerged from this was rooted in my new myth of King Arthur. I realized that there was no separation between what was right as a personal conviction and what was right as a public position. By believing that I could maintain consistency, that I could respect others and act from integrity, I was able to see that each and every moment presented me with the chance to be conscious of my greater self. I made the effort to consider each major decision within the context of finding the most compassionate course to follow.

Where I had once believed that I could not act out of my inner values, I came to realize that not doing so created a contradiction between my inner compass and my outward behavior. Healing the gap between what I thought was right and how I acted was most important. I was far less effective when I allowed the fear of how I would be judged to inhibit me from doing what I saw to be true to my inner lights. Sometimes my only choice was between the lesser of evils, but usually the greater good was available.

My path to growth had been painful, but it led me deep into myself. The awareness that consciousness co-creates external circumstances continued to guide me. I was not an observer or an object being acted on. I was one with the creative energy of the cosmos, participating in the shaping of the world.

I became aware of how powerful my thoughts and intentions were. My enlightenment about the equal plane that existed between my inner psyche and my external world became one of the pillars of my spirituality.

5

Light from the Sky

Every child needs to hear:
You came out of the energy
That gave birth to the Universe
It is your beginning.
You came out of the fire
That fashioned the galaxies:
It is alive within you.
—Brian Swimme

WHEN I REALIZED that I had internalized a story that affected how I thought, I gained a new respect for story. Because of my belief that I was the hero of my story, I had been responding to the world out of that assumed archetype since childhood. My hero story shaped the way I saw the world, and determined how I reacted to it. What became clear was that my inner belief about my identity conditioned how I thought about the outer world.

With this discovery, I was able to consider whether that story still served me. My breakthrough into consciousness was enlivening. I saw that my inner and outer worlds were not separate at all, but were integrated. I had chosen to pursue conflict in the external world in order to enable myself to resolve the conflicts that persisted within me. What better arena could I find to work out authority conflicts than a form in which, every two years, I had to go up against the government—the ultimate archetype of authority—and test myself as the hero. It was a struggle driven by my ego, which itself was a construct of my own mind.

I contemplated my new enlightenment. What could I learn from the power of the mind to create reality? Was I really in control of my thoughts and actions, or were there other outside filters that influenced how I thought? I began to wonder if my culture had a mythos. Did humanity have a collective myth? Was there a story buried in our collective subconscious that was parallel to my personal one?

In the early 1990s, I was only just becoming aware of the seriousness of the environmental crisis. Jack Munro, the Canadian head of the International Woodworkers of America, was a colleague and a fellow vice president of Federation of Labor. His union was coming under pressure for the practices of the companies logging the coast. There was growing controversy about the logging of the pristine, original-growth forests on the West Coast. The environmental movement was mounting strong opposition to clear-cut logging and was lobbying to ban logging in many untouched watersheds.

The largest company of that time, MacMillan Bloedel, was mounting a targeted defense of its activities. Jack invited me to take a helicopter tour of the wild western coast of Vancouver Island, to see firsthand what both the company and his union members were doing.

That trip had the opposite effect on me to the one that Jack had intended. I was shocked and disturbed by the destruction of huge tracts of ancient trees. My spirit rebelled at the sight of giant Douglas fir trees lying dead on the ground. The attitude of the forester who was our guide seemed to be that these trees were simply resources for his company, there to be cut down so that humans could give them value. The loggers echoed this attitude. But I saw the heart of the crisis. Like the environmentalists, I saw the trees as living entities, with the right to life and protection. Instead of supporting the company and the loggers, I returned from that tour squarely on the side of nature.

As I was coming to grips with the environmental crisis, I realized how the powerfully the biblical myth of Adam and Eve still influences modern thinking. The creation story from Genesis shaped the worldview of the West. What child has not heard of the Garden of Eden? In the Garden, God is pictured as giving Adam dominance over all creation. "God blessed them; and God said to them, 'Be fruitful and multiply, and fill the earth, and subdue it; and *rule over the fish of the sea and over the birds of the sky and over every living thing that moves on the earth.*'"[1]

Two beliefs overlap and reinforce each other. The first belief is that the Bible is God speaking to humankind, and therefore the text is infallibly true. The second is that humans are separate from nature and were give the world as theirs to do with it as they chose.

[1] (Gen. 1:28 New American Standard Version)

Taken literally as God's will, this story gives humans permission to exploit the world.

By placing everything in the world at the disposal of humans, Christianity has fostered the attitudes that have led to today's environmental crisis. St. Augustine, in the fifth century of the Common Era, used the Adam and Eve story to declare the world sinful. In the seventeenth century, John Locke used the literal interpretation of the story to justify the private ownership of property. The Church has used the story to support its condemnation of Galileo and its dismissal of Darwin. The literal reading of Genesis has pitted religion against science for several hundred years. Believing the mandate in the Garden to be true, Christianity has embedded its interpretation of Genesis into Western consciousness, as well as influenced the development of capitalism and liberalism in Europe and its colonies. The representatives of the forestry companies and the loggers both believed that they were divinely sanctioned to use the environment for their benefit.

I thought about the biblical story of creation the evening when I first heard Dr. Brian Swimme describe the discoveries scientists had recently made about the universe. I was hearing a new story, one that did not yet make sense to me.

Swimme was introduced to the audience as a cosmologist. I did not really know what a scientific cosmologist was, although I had studied cosmology in philosophy classes in the seminary. I knew that cosmology played a very large part in shaping the worldview of the authors of the Bible. The assumptions people made about the universe showed up in the way the biblical writers described the world. The earth was thought to be small and flat, and the heavens were a solid dome over the earth, not too far above the mountains.

But the young Californian Swimme described a very different vision of the universe. He spoke eloquently and enthusiastically about the wonders that scientists had uncovered as they studied the evidence of the Big Bang.

Swimme brought the cosmic origin alive. I found his excitement about these new discoveries contagious, and while I listened to him talk about the new cosmology, I remembered what I knew of the ancient one. He commented that everyone who had ever lived assumed that the universe had always been like we see it now. The Bible's authors believed that God had created the world as is, Swimme noted, and the creation story inferred that it was a perfect paradise in the beginning but that humans were responsible for all pain and suffering.

Secular scientists assumed that the universe was eternal and unchanging, and for the most of Western history, humans had accepted that story. They had no idea that it could change. Swimme recalled that when Albert Einstein began to explore light, time, and space, he concluded that movement of light indicated that the universe should be expanding. After the American astronomer Edwin Hubble showed Einstein that the universe was indeed expanding in every direction, Einstein declared that the universe had begun from a single energy event, but at the time—in the early twentieth century—there was no way to prove his theory.

Swimme told his audience that in the mid-1960s two scientists at Bell Laboratories in New Jersey had accidentally discovered evidence that confirmed Einstein's theory about the universe's origin.

Arno Penzias and Robert W. Wilson found static coming from everywhere in the universe, and won the Nobel Prize in Physics in 1978 by realizing that they were observing the remnants of the birth of the universe—the very event that Einstein had described. The universe had exploded into being in a single energy event, and all previous assumptions about the nature of the cosmos would gradually be erased by this discovery.

NASA became very curious about Penzias and Wilson's discovery, known as the Cosmic Microwave Background, and assigned scientists to explore the evidence. In 1989, NASA launched a probe, dubbed the Cosmic Background Explorer (COBE), to search the heavens for traces of the radiation suspected to come from the originating event. Once the information from COBE had been analyzed, NASA released the images, which turned out to be the most important images in all of human history, changing irrevocably the way humanity thought about the universe and everything in it. These images confirmed that the universe indeed had a beginning and, from the outset, was capable of evolving. NASA's work set off the development of a new cosmology that would eclipse all previous understandings of the universe.

Images like this one (Figure 1) provided conclusive evidence for the Big Bang. American scientists were then convinced of the birth of the universe. NASA's press release said:

In essence, the satellite, launched in November 1989, has peered back in time to detect the now faint whispers of the Big Bang that is widely believed to have started the expansion of the universe about fifteen billion years ago. "What we've done is to measure the microwave radiation that comes to us almost equally from every direction and that is thought to be the primary remnant of the Big Bang," said [Dr. John] Mather.

Figure 1. Cosmic Microwave Background (NASA)

As Swimme painted a picture of the startling change in humanity's understanding of the origin of the cosmos, these new concepts shook my own understanding of the universe to its foundations.

Although I didn't know it at the time, Swimme was reopening the door to spirituality for me. I would need several more years and a lot more study to integrate what I heard that night, but the new story of the cosmic origins was so new and different that it completely transformed my understanding of reality.

Swimme's mentor, Father Thomas Berry, perceived the continuing energy event as both spiritual and material, and offered a profoundly spiritual understanding of the originating event. Together, Swimme and Father Berry introduced me to a transformative understanding of the origin and nature of the cosmos. The scope and depth of the new perspective shifted my consciousness, completely reorienting my psychic compass. The image from NASA meant that everything that is now in the universe arose from that initial flaring of energy. I began to understand that the cosmos is evolutionary, gradually developing one stage at a time. It is a unitary entity, and it is acting.

That evening, Father Berry described the amazing evolutionary process of cosmogenesis, the revolutionary idea that the universe is self-generating, producing its own unfolding from within its internal dynamic. No external force or influence is possible. Everything in the universe emerges from it. There is no outside or before.

The initiating thermonuclear eruption created elementary particles that began a chain reaction of development. In the beginning, every particle was exposed to every other particle, setting up a field of connection where everything is in unity. The incipient universe contained all of the seeds that would flower over time to become this earth, the Milky Way Galaxy, all the billions of galaxies, and the billions of stars in each galaxy. The universe, emerging from the scattered waves of energy evolved into the far-flung array of stars and galaxies now in existence.

I paid especially close attention to the parallels between the creative process of the universe's unfolding from within its essence and the power of my consciousness to create my own reality. Berry used the phrase "the new story" to describe the flowing narrative of the unfolding universe. It was unexpected to see a priest be so comfortable with new developments replacing the ancient story that had been so formative of Western thinking. But Berry explained it this way: The idea of story, he said, conveys the notion of a single ongoing narrative that remains finished. He surprised me with his openness to a scientific understanding of the unfolding cosmos, as well as his reliance on new information to augment the biblical way of describing the beginning.

The idea of story appealed strongly to me. It's easy to get lost in the emerging technical science, but the meaning of that information is universally accessible. Like the universe, I too had been evolving, and each turn in my path was an opportunity to grow— and my growth was continually taking me into new territory.

Like Teilhard de Chardin, who had opened my eyes many years ago to the depth of spiritual fire in the cosmos, Berry offered me new eyes with which to view evolving nature. His inspired writings on the emergence of the conscious spiritual energy provided me with a new way of grasping the meaning of ongoing creativity.

As I kept learning more about the cosmologists' findings, I would excitedly tell my associates and friends about it, as if it were the latest installment in a good TV serial. For many reasons, I was fascinated by this story, which unites science and spirit, and its implications, both for me and for the world. Suddenly, scientists sounded like mystics. The scientific visionaries who had gone beyond the paradigm of a material cosmos described energy as conscious and spirit filled. The new proponents of the profound mystery were bringing fact and mystery together.

In the past, most scientists shied away from the nonmaterial, but the theologians were so deeply rooted in their religious tradition that they were blind to the more wondrous implications of the information coming from science. Today we cannot speak about the nature of the universe without including spirit, meaning, and purpose.

Because of science, humanity's perception of the universe has changed completely. We are now in a time of transition. The worldview that emerged from the materialistic cosmology still holds sway over our collective imagination, but thanks to science, that worldview has been proven false. The new story is directing us away from a mechanistic view of the universe. I hope that the earth and the environment will benefit from our turning away from false, materialistic beliefs about the world. it is urgent that we embrace the implication of a conscious cosmos, and change our destructive ways of living on earth.

If our previous fundamental assumptions about the nature of the universe were wrong, then every conclusion we have drawn from those assumption would be flawed. Certainly, the cosmology that was prevalent when religions were developed has been proven false, and the replacement assumption, namely that of the material, mechanical universe, has been shown to be equally flawed. Unraveling the grip of the materialistic worldview is a gargantuan task, yet, for the sake of the environment and the planet, we must rapidly change our minds.

Humanity is being shown a self-generating universe, one that is a single energy event. Everything that has ever existed is part of the evolutionary dynamic of the cosmos. At our most fundamental level, we share identity with all other creatures in nature. We are united and one. Everything is knit together as one, therefore any act against nature is a violation of our own being.

How can we continue to despoil our world for our own gain

when we now know that by doing so, we are contaminating parts of ourselves? It is a violation of our very nature to harm the natural world.

I believe that I am in the universe to continue and to foster the development of the unfolding earth. My deepest nature wants to be aligned with whatever enhances life on earth. The clearer I get about my oneness with the earth and with all creation, the more I know myself. I experience myself with an urgent sense of responsibility to stop the destruction, but at the same time, I am at peace, knowing that I am of the universe, and one with the All.

The universe is constantly creating the present moment, and the expansion of space/time is progressing, regenerating one moment at a time. This is an enormous spiritual lesson. The only time is *now*. This is the only time there is, and in it is the entire evolution from the beginning of the Big Bang, 13.7 billion years ago. The entire evolutionary history points to this present moment. Now, therefore, is the most significant point in space/time. What an auspicious moment to be alive!

Because this is the culmination of cosmic history, it is the fruition of the cosmogenesis. The universe has evolved to this moment. While there is a great deal of chance, there is no sense of accident. The universe is directing evolution. I ask myself, why am I in this moment? Every thing I do comes from how I understand the answer.

The best new science, along with the best of the spiritual wisdom of the ages, suggests that we are in this moment to contribute our unique gifts to the great unfolding. We come out of the universe to play a role in the unfolding of the universe. This is the opposite of meaninglessness.

The cosmos is a matrix from which everything flows. Those describing the cosmos could be speaking of a "thou" rather than an "it." I regard the matrix with reverence, and see in it the sacred nature of the Great Mother, and I espouse the emerging perception that the cosmos is a living entity. To me, the universe is a radiant, expanding reality. I see myself within it, and of it. This discovery has galvanized my identification with the sacred nature of everything.

For more than twenty years, after I abandoned the religious orientation that came from Christianity, I searched for the key to a spiritual understanding. The biblical story has been augmented by new revelation. I realize that I was never fully comfortable with the materialistic view. With the emerging worldview, an entirely different template is available thanks to the scientific information provided by NASA and the cosmologists. I feel solidly anchored as part of the unfolding cosmos. My renewed spirituality requires that I see that this moment has been cooking since the beginning of time. I believe that, as a result, I am in this time and this place in order to play a specific role in the continuing unfolding of the cosmos. I have been developing a greater self-awareness, becoming more conscious of what I am bringing into the creative process.

What I bring into this moment is a manifestation of cosmic intention. I have come to see that the increase of my consciousness is connected to an unfolding awareness within the cosmos. If the universe is truly one, then my consciousness and the universe are also one. Could it be that my questions are the universe exploring itself?

My questions about the environment and the future health of the planet come together with the wisdom that comes from an ancient connection to nature. My thirst for social justice, to see an end to abject poverty, to the equal distribution of clean water, for an end to disregard of infant mortality and maternal health, is connected to my sense of responsibility in this moment to the well-being of the whole. I yearn for an end to war and the causes of war. Each new inquiry leads to increasing consciousness, which in turn leads to greater curiosity about how to make the world work better. The resulting insights plunge me deeply into mystery.

Consciousness, both individually and collectively, is key to the new view of the cosmos, and is analogous to the background radiation that originates from the Big Bang. It shows up as a quality in everything at its deepest level, and researchers have discovered that it is present at the most minute quantum level. Consciousness, which has been prized by spiritual seers throughout history, is turning out to be a fundamental property of the cosmos.

In fact, scientists tell us that the universe itself is determining the rate of expansion of the elements forged in the Big Bang. The relationships and ratios determined in the first instant of the emergence of cosmic energy indicates that the universe chose how it would expand. The rate of expansion determined the formation of galaxies, which in turn continue to generate new stars in the hundreds of billions. The evidence available from the Hubble Space Telescope shows that this is an ongoing process.

A flood of discoveries has yielded insights into the properties of the heavens, and these revelations are profound, but what shines out from all the work done on this new story is that everything in the universe is interconnected. There is growing evidence that no element or particle exists disconnected from all other matter. Indeed, the evidence is now convincing that the universe is generating itself from the single source, and that the energy that gave rise to the first galaxy is still animating life on earth today. Everything that exists participates in a single web of being. All of the dazzling diversity of minerals, animals, and plants that make up the earth arise out of earth. As members of the Earth community, we are of the universe and an integral part of a cosmic whole.

6

The Call of the Wild

The most beautiful thing we can experience is the mysterious.
It is the source of all true art and all science. He to whom this
emotion is a stranger, who can no longer pause to wonder
and stand rapt in awe, is as good as dead: his eyes are closed.
—Albert Einstein

A s I WRITE, it is 2011 and I am living in Victoria, British Columbia, on the shore of the Pacific Ocean. From my front windows, I can look across the Straight of Juan de Fuca at the snow-capped Olympic Mountains in the State of Washington. The city of Victoria was originally Salish territory but settlers established a fur-trading outpost and a staging place for the Cariboo Gold Rush, which began in 1858. As one of the oldest cities on the West Coast, Victoria has retained its original beauty and charm. In less than a thirty-minute drive, I can be in a pastoral countryside, and an hour travel brings me into dense forest at the foothills of the mountains. Whether I am by the open sea or in the ancient forest, I am conscious of my connection to the surrounding natural world.

Ever since I first settled here, I have been aware that First

Nations communities dot the surrounding shore and countryside. I consider myself fortunate to be enriched by aboriginal culture and art, which reminds me that the land I now call home has been occupied for thousands of years by people indigenous to this place.

The stunning beauty of the environment keeps me conscious of my close connection to nature. Though I live in the city, I also live in close proximity to the wild.

Every day I see the migrating sea birds, the whales, and the eagles in every season. Because of this, I have grown in my concern for what we are doing to this fragile planet. I worry that it may be too late to restore the balance, and the environmental crisis has become a spiritual crisis for me.

On a rainy November day several years ago, I gathered with a group of fifteen men from a spirituality circle that I had been facilitating for a good many years. Deep in the rainforest of Canada's Pacific Northwest, we had come from our comfortable homes to explore how we could reconnect with nature. Some of us were from urban centers, others from rural communities. At that time, I lived in a rural setting on a coastal island. The purpose for our gathering was our common interest in being more connected with the natural world. We acknowledged that human-dominated life patterns had replaced or obscured nature's rhythms, making us become disconnected from Earth. We also acknowledged that we had become reliant on the built environment at the expense of our primal relationship to the natural world. We were asking ourselves if we had all traded spiritual wellbeing for material comfort, and acknowledged that along with feeling isolated from the natural world, we were also feeling out of harmony within ourselves. That weekend we wanted to revive our deep connection to the wild.

On the first night of our gathering, an elder from a local native community reminded us that the aboriginal people had prospered in that land. They knew the cycles of nature, and when and where to harvest the abundant plant and marine life. Locally abundant foods once fed an entire village, and were harvested with respect and with an understanding of the recurring cycles of growth and migration. The elder told us that among the First Nations, the expression "All my relations" was not limited to family. Instead, it recognized kinship of all the elements of nature as well as the human presence. The worldview of the aboriginal people encompassed everything that supported life. Even the rocks were called the "grandmothers" because they contained the wisdom of the ages.

Living in harmony with the natural world was central to the elder's teaching. This tenet is at the heart of the way First Peoples around the globe live and practice their core values. Aboriginal people do not think of themselves as separate from land or sea. From the tip of Peru to the Arctic tundra, native people revere the land and have done so for millennia because they have a relationship with the world that sustains them.

When I was head of the union, the provincial and federal governments appointed me as a labor representative to the Treaty Negotiation Advisory Committee. The committee—composed of business, government, labor, and environmental leaders—had the responsibility to advise government about how treaty proposals would affect various interests in the province.

During our deliberations, I witnessed the clash between the

descendants of European colonizers and British Columbia's First Nations. As the committee reviewed the impact of future treaties on the fish, mining, and forestry industries, corporate sector representatives refused to accept any claim that the First Peoples had to the wealth of the land they had lived on for thousands of years. The people who now controlled the logging and fishing industries, did everything they could to block the First Nations from regaining their rights to prosperity.

I had not witnessed such raw racism since being involved in the Civil Rights struggle in America's South. For thousands of years, the First Nations had lived off their harvest of salmon and shellfish. They now were denied the right to catch fish in their traditional territories for food and ceremony. As though they were invisible, the aboriginal people were expected to prove that they had a right to exist to the people who had moved into their traditional territories.

At that time, I was just discovering my place in the cosmos, and the emerging thinking was that everything and everyone on the earth had a common origin in the evolution of the planet. *We are all one.* The deeply spiritual implication of our oneness was beginning to sink in.

I had been raised to trust that my senses were an accurate reflection of the world, and I was just beginning to question whether my senses are in fact a reliable representation of the reality all around me. Since the early part of the twentieth century, quantum physicists had been saying that the subatomic world was strangely dissimilar from the world we perceive. But now the Cosmic Background Explorer Mission (COBE) was in the process of confirming that the vast universe is primarily energy. What we see is not solid, neither at the microscopic level nor in the macro scale. The scattered galaxies and stars in the night sky are a template for the atomic and molecular pattern below the visible scale. I could not understand why we do not perceive energy and why the human senses mask the fact that the universe is alive with consciousness and spirit, which the new discoveries told us was indeed the case.

I was coming to understand that it is necessary to understand how essentially one we are with the entire universe. We cannot look at trees and salmon as merely being resources that are there for our use. Our consciousness has to change to come into alignment with the reality of the universe.

The Maya of Middle America see themselves as connecting the heart of the sky with the heart of the earth. Their cosmology is holistic and their worldview integrates man and nature. By holding to their cosmology and worldview, the Maya have endured in the face of overwhelming pressure to conform to Western values. Their sense of unity with the world was alien to the European settlers who came to the New World and attempted to "civilize" them.[1]

As we struggle to reclaim our relationship to nature, the nature-based spirituality of the Maya is a clue to what is possible. If we examine the ways that our contemporary society's views differ from the views of the First Peoples, we can pinpoint where they diverge. The original peoples of this land knew they depended on the fish, the caribou, and the buffalo for their sustenance and survival. They valued the diversity of plant life and the animals they lived among,

[1] Dr. Robin June Hood, *A Curriculum of Place and Respect: Towards an Understanding of Contemporary Mayan Education*, University of Victoria, (unpublished doctoral thesis)

and when they drew on these for food and medicinal healing, they did so with respect. Over thousands of years, they developed a balanced relationship with the animals and plants of both the land and the sea. Out of this age-old realization of the interdependence of human with nature, the First Peoples evolved a worldview that sustained them.

In Canada, the local First Nations hold nature with reverence. For them, the human presence in the world is one with the whole, and not experienced as separated from the environment. The people who first inhabited the wild places saw themselves as essential to the interplay of elements. I have come to realize how powerful a role cosmology plays in the way everyone sees and reacts to the world.

Until recently, our society showed no signs of challenging its worldview. What is changing now is the growing number of people who want to take part in what environmental activist and Buddhist scholar Joanna Macy calls the Great Turning. The number of people who are tapping into the spirituality of the earth continues to grow. We are witnessing one of the greatest transformations in thinking in centuries.

At the men's retreat I organized in the rainforest of Canada's Pacific Northwest, at a lodge that stood among the giant trees in the Sooke Hills, the elder used stories and parables to illustrated his teachings and life lessons. His stories had come down by word of mouth from generation to generation. Together, we sat in a circle before a huge stone fireplace as he offered us his wisdom. I was mesmerized by the blazing fire. The flames carried my imagination beyond the large hall into far-flung communities in the wilderness.

In my mind, I stood beside hunters and fishers dwelling in harmony with their surroundings.

"How did we fall out of connection with nature?" one man in the circle asked. Was it really progress to wind up alienated from the natural world? Our generation, as so many before us, was formed by a worldview that placed no value on the environment or the natural world. The worldview we inherited believed the material world had no inherent value, spirit, or importance except as resource for human needs. Like the ancient worldview before it, the materialist view placed humans at the top of the pyramid. We have all been educated to take for granted that everything is at our disposal, and twenty-one centuries of Western thinking have cemented our view.

In the group, I acknowledged that for much of my life I too had taken the environment for granted. I had seen it as merely being there to be used, its resources to be exploited. Indeed, I had even once believed there was nothing to be learned from a lifeless cosmos.

The other men who sat around the fire with me agreed that we were being impoverished by our separation from a deep connection to the earth. We mused about how the human community had changed. In the beginning, people had depended on nature and lived in harmony with the environment, respecting the other members of the earth community as fellow creatures. One man in the group even spoke about the very real possibility that humanity could destroy life on earth, and sounded the alarm about the dangers of how far we have already strained the quality of environmental health. He warned us that we were causing the greatest eradication of species since the extinction of the dinosaurs, sixty-five million years ago, and pointed out that we were doing this by the way we treated the earth's essential elements: air, water, and soil. He asked if any of us could show any evidence that humans have benefited any other species on earth beside themselves.

The scope and scale of humanity's pillaging of the earth is so huge that my mind could not cope with the magnitude of the issue. I had heard stories of how many trees were being cut down each day in Africa or South America, and in my own region, I had seen truckloads of ancient trees cut down and destined for shipment to other parts of the world. Sometimes it seemed as if the overwhelming scale of the destruction numbed me to my responsibility for it as a consumer. I began to ask myself: What does my lifestyle contribute to spreading pollution into the air we breathe, our vital waterways, and the increasingly depleted nutrients in the soil?

I had recently seen a news report telling of whales gone missing from local pods. Seven to ten whales were presumed to have starved to death. Was there a connection between the pollution of the ocean and the loss of the whales? Was the disappearance of salmon from our waters the result of bad aquacultural management or global warming? Or was there some other reason that we did not yet know?

We also talked about a headline from a few years earlier, which baldly stated that a study from the U.S. concluded that only ten percent of the ocean's fish remain. One fisherman in the group told us that the oceans are dying because of human abuse, and yet we resist taking the necessary steps to conserve and preserve them. Humans refuse to accept the direct connection between the decline in the life systems of our planet and our behavior. How am I connected to the dying off of salmon and whales? And how am I affecting the bears and eagles that rely on those fish for their diets?

Mine was not a new awareness. I had begun feeling the Earth's plight when I left the priesthood and returned to British Columbia from Texas. The experience of abandoning the clergy, rejecting my religion, and leaving a place where I had been known and honored had triggered a profound sense of loss. When I came to my new home in Victoria, I did not feel very connected to the place. I was longing for somewhere else. The dissonance I felt permeated everything in my life: my new marriage, my work, my relationship with my mother and father in New York, even my friends from the Paulist Fathers and from Austin were all affected. I looked at life through the prism of loss, resentment, and loneliness. I had never before felt such a strong sense of estrangement. The suffering environment became a symbol for my inner state of being.

I heard Joanna Macy speak when I was the executive director of a retreat center on Gabriola Island in British Columbia called The Haven. Joanna made an impression on me when she advised the retreat attendees not to quell the anguish and pain they felt at what is happening to the natural world. If we did, she said, we would dull ourselves to being in the reality. We cannot participate in the Great Turning unless we are fully aware and connected to the plight of the natural world.

Three extraordinary First Nations leaders became my friends as well as my teachers. Each one taught me about being a leader who integrated place, environment, and a determination for justice: Joe Gosnell, chief of the Nisga'a Nation; Joe Mathias, chief of the Squamish Nation; and George Watt, chief of the Nuu-chah-nulth and founder of the Nuu-chah-nulth Tribal Council. I was privileged to know each of the chiefs from three quite different Nations. Each of them held a conviction that their people could come into harmony with the society that had come to settle in their territories, provided that their fundamental rights were acknowledged. Each of them was a traditional leader in the tribal lineage of their own First Nation, and each one was a spiritual person deeply connected to the Earth.

Chief Joe Gosnell, the heredity leader of the Nisga'a people in the rugged Nass River valley in northern British Columbia, invited me to visit him in his home village. One day, as we took a walk there, he pointed to a mountain and told me that he derived his identity from it. I saw a profound relationship between man and place. Chief Gosnell's spiritual strength is rooted in the place where his people have lived for ten thousand years. This was one of the clearest examples of strong connection between people and the natural world. What I took away from my relationship with him was that aboriginal spirituality is imbedded in places as well as in nature. Chief Gosnell showed me that we cannot stand apart from nature and look at it as though it is different from ourselves. When humans study nature, they are within the context rather than apart from it. But quantum mechanics long ago proved that the observer is part of the field of study. Contemporary cosmology reinforces that we are within the whole. Humanity is a product of the evolving universe. There is no outside from which to study nature, and indigenous people have always known this.

The limitation of the Western religious tradition was that it taught that humans were only passing through this world. In the second and third centuries, religious thinkers did not know that we are actually of the universe. To them, attaining life meant leaving the Earth for a heaven in the sky. Today, many religious scholars, like Mary Ellen Tucker, are embracing the notion and have a radical responsibility for the Earth.

The most empirical study of cosmology concludes that the energy that gives rise to all material in the universe is conscious, and has been from the first instant of its manifestation. With the presence of consciousness comes what we call spirit. Consequently, human spirituality must be rooted in the Earth.

Personally, I know my spirituality through my bodily senses. I cannot be spiritual in my head alone. I cannot care for the whales if I only look at them as being different, and separate from me. I am one with the whales in one complex fabric, because we are the Earth community. Spirituality that is not grounded in the stuff of the Earth is ephemeral and unengaged. Science shows us that we have been produced by the slow process of evolution over billions of years. That takes away any temptation to be haughty or remain apart from the flow of energy as it pushes forward as the universe moving toward its completion.

Consciousness is the source of the human ability to perceive the more-than-material nature of the world in which we live, and consciousness of place is key to indigenous spirituality. In Buddhism, consciousness is the element of experience that the Buddha identified as enlightenment. For me, consciousness was the illumination that transformed my subconscious mythology into a more relevant one, and I now see consciousness as a constituent of everything in the universe. The energy that brought the cosmos into what we know it to be is consciousness.

After I retired from the union, I began to work with men who wanted to explore spirituality in their lives. Every Wednesday evening, we met in a circle, which is a very powerful setting, because it is both a container and a distributor of energy. As I write, more than ten years later, our Wednesday Spirituality group is still meeting. At the outset, we agreed to some guidelines to make the setting a safe one within which to share deep thoughts. We agreed to meet to explore our spirituality, and that spirit showed up in respect. We would treat each other with respect. We would listen with a full concentration whenever anyone else was speaking. We would not interrupt or contradict anyone, or act as though we had a better idea or understood something better than anyone else. In that atmosphere, thoughts and reflections are best expressed in the first person, from one's own experience. Someone else's experience cannot be contradicted. If they share what is in their heart, they are offering gold.

Over the years, men have reached into their depths to share, be heard, and be healed, and some profound sharing has taken place. When someone new joins the circle, they are asked if they will subscribe to the agreements of the group. The circle models the behavior that has become characteristic of the group. The safe environment allows what was inner to come to the fore. I am always amazed at how deep men will go in that environment.

In a circle, conscious awareness occurs in an environment of safety, and is enhanced when we experience acceptance. The bridge between the heart and the mind, the inner and the outer is supported within the circle when people commit to being together with respect. I suspect that the qualities that are accessed in the circle, although rare in our interactions with one another, make a profound difference to our experience. The circle is a place of intention, and one defined by ritual. We begin each evening by experiencing a few minutes in silence, shedding the stresses of our day, and then we go round the circle, expressing gratitude for something in our lives. We conclude the evening with another round of appreciation expressed for someone or something that happened in the circle.

I have always experienced the circle as spiritual. Its energy is palpable. The intention to attend to each other with respect allows us to reveal ourselves in a spirit of open-heartedness. Because we are connected, we are able to embrace the spirit of each person speaking as if that os the most important thing we can do at that moment. In our circle, these tangible experience of unity and caring have fostered peace and healing.

The circle is the traditional symbol of spirit. As I have noted, the aboriginal people do all of their significant deliberations while sitting in a circle. And according to the Arthurian legend, King Arthur met with his knights at a roundtable, which communicated a sense of equality with the king to all. In the spirit of unity that the circle conveys, Arthur sent his companions on their quests from the roundtable.

I believe that consciousness is the portal to spirituality, and it is a state that can be developed in everyone. In my development, my greatest impetus to consciousness was meditation. The form I chose was Transcendental Meditation, taught by the Maharishi Mahesh Yogi.

Once I accepted that the universe is unfolding with consciousness, I realized that there is purposefulness in the evolutionary chaos. In fact, the universe is selecting its own direction, spiraling toward a final and divine unification, which French Jesuit priest Pierre Teilhard de Chardin called the Omega Point.

In the circle, we replicate the shape of the galaxies and the form of the creation of the stars. It takes an open heart to see the spiritual significance in symbols such as the circle, and to know that these symbols lead us into the mystery of cosmic self-creation.

The journey to spirit is a journey into mystery. Spirit is not found in the concrete, although we discover it through our earthly bodies. Peter Russell, a theoretical physicist and mystic, sees the evidence of spirit at the inception of the universe in the identification of spirit and light. They share the same properties, he says, and both are present in the tumult of the cauldron of elements that produces the emerging cosmos[2]. I am attracted to the likening of consciousness and light in the universe at the metaphoric and transcendental level of cosmic unfolding.

o o o

The universe that is revealing itself to us in the evidence of the new cosmos is so much more wonderful than anything than even the most advanced seers could perceive. And yet it is not beyond our understanding. On the contrary, the cosmos invites us to enter its

[2] Peter Russell, *From Science to God, The Mystery of Consciousness and the Meaning of Light*, Novato, California: New World Library, 2003.

mystery and imbibe the majesty of its nature. The cosmos is beyond our reckoning in its full dimension. We are likely to find ourselves in rapture of its dimensions for ages to come.

And, in both a scientific and a poetic sense, we *are* the universe. The universe is in us, in the sense that we manifest it in all its majesty. We are the universe reflecting on itself, as we explore the ramifications of what it is revealing.

The cosmic revolution that began with the image of cosmic radiation is only just starting to show its implications. Meanwhile, collectively, we are only just beginning to grasp the meaning of what we are being shown. With each new insight, we are being challenged to abandon all the flawed concepts that are unworthy of the universe that is revealing itself to us.

As I write, I am struggling to integrate the scientific knowledge that is coming at a prodigious rate with the expansion of my consciousness, generated by this new information, and the insights that accompany each new discovery. Likewise, I am working to keep all of that in the context of spirit and humility. The most exciting aspect of this moment is that we are able to participate, right from the beginning, in this new phase of cosmic evolution.

7

Life and Death in
the Unfolding Cosmos

Tell me, what else should I have done?
Doesn't everything die at last and too soon?
Tell me, what is it you plan to do
With your one wild and precious life?[1]
—Mary Oliver

MY EXPERIENCES OF the deaths of my father and my mother both happened at a time before I was fully awake to my emotional life. That did not mute the pain I felt at their loss. Each of those deaths was a catastrophic loss that pushed me toward the brink of my own mortality. I am an only child, and after my parents' deaths, I felt like an orphan.

I was still not yet forty when my mother died. She appeared to have a stroke, rapidly losing her capacity to speak and, finally, the use of her wonderful mind. She was admitted to a nursing home in Southampton with what turned out to be cancer of the brain.

[1] Mary Oliver, A Summer Day

Her deterioration occurred in only eight months. I drove across the continent five times to see her during her decline, and each visit left me full of anguish.

Usually Madeleine accompanied me on those visits. During one visit, when we arrived at the nursing home, even though my mother no longer had the ability to speak, she still glared at Madeleine with unvarnished hatred when she noticed her there with me. I could only assume that my mother's early opinion, which was that Madeleine was responsible for my leaving the priesthood and moving to the West Coast, had resurfaced with fresh blame and resentment.

I was deeply conflicted. On the one hand, If my mother had been able to talk, I would have defended my wife from her. As it was, Madeleine recoiled from the look, and I knew she suffered from it.

But I also felt compassion for my mother and her condition, and I wanted to bring her to Victoria so that I could comfort her and see her more often. She was not in physical pain, but she had gradually lost conscious connection to the world around her. But her doctor did not want her moved. It was not until after my mother's death that her doctor revealed that the cause of her death had been brain cancer. I had not known the extent of her suffering, for it was not on the outside.

I distanced myself from feeling the effect of my mother's death, and became numb to the loss. It took many years of inner struggle before I was able to mourn her passing fully. I loved her and missed her, yet at the same time, I resented the way she could use her emotions to control mine.

Twenty years after my mother's death, Madeleine was diagnosed with an incurable form of lymphoma. I already knew very well what the death of a loved one felt like, so I anticipated the pain of loss. The prospect of Madeleine's death reawakened in me the traumatic experiences of childhood abandonment—early-life experiences that were lodged in my primitive brain. Even though I had cleared the memory out of my muscles, where it had blocked the free flow of my energy, my reptilian brain was reacting to the prospect of Madeleine's loss, and reading it as abandonment.

Five years passed from Madeleine's initial diagnosis to the point at which her lymphoma symptoms became debilitating. In the late 1990s, tumors showed up all over her body, and her health began to fail in other ways.

Madeleine had strong views about the available options for cancer patients. She called the treatments, "cut, burn, or poison," and did not want to participate in any of them, especially since, in her case, there was no clear likelihood they would cure the cancer. She was not interested in simply prolonging life in a state of debilitation. I was not as sanguine about her not availing herself of the best of medical science, but I could not prevail over her conviction about how to care for herself.

When she thought that she might be helped by an energy treatment that she had read about in a book on alternative treatments, we invested in a light beam generator from the United States, and I underwrote the cost of having a local couple who were energy medicine practitioners learn the protocols for using it effectively. To my amazement, over the course of four months, the tumors shrunk as the practitioner applied the light beam in conjunction with lymph massage.

At one point, I thought that Madeleine would not live out the year, and began making plans to step down from the presidency of the union. She was adamant that as long as there were signs of her improvement, I should continue my job. Mary Maxwell, a friend of Madeleine who is a trained nurse, moved from Saskatoon to Victoria to be with her. Mary came to our home every day for months to look after Madeleine's practical needs. Although Madeleine's cancer seemed to be going into remission, I told the union I would not be seeking reelection for another term.

After a heartwarming send-off at the union's convention, I shifted my energy from the broad stage of union leadership to the very specific stage of caring for another person. The change was more difficult than I suspected. For many years, I had maintained an apartment in Vancouver, close to the union's headquarters, and lived there part-time. Now I packed up both my office and my apartment and relocated full-time to our home in Victoria.

Madeleine had often described our living arrangement as ideal for marriage between middle-aged people. I was free to devote all my energy to my work, without needing to attend to anyone else's needs or schedule. For Madeleine, the quiet of an undisturbed environment at home allowed her to paint and teach.

She had adopted the painting of mandalas as her primary art form and spiritual practice. After returning to art school in the early 1980s, she studied with Jack Wise, a well-known West Coast painter, who had adapted the Tibetan Buddhist mandala by substituting inner psychological symbols for the religious iconography of Tibet. He combined the depth exploration of Jung and the Buddhist discipline that lamas practiced in the painting of their religious mandalas.

When Madeleine began painting the mandalas at home, she attracted students. In addition to the Buddhist discipline of paying one hundred percent attention to the tip of the brush, and letting the subject emerge rather than imposing a form on the paper, Madeleine introduced a journaling practice that evoked the personal significance of the images that emerged. She valued quiet because she needed to do her work in contemplative silence.

When I came home to become her caregiver, we both had to make major adjustments. I did not realize the extent to which I carried the union and the political environment of the province within my psyche. I was constantly scanning the horizon for threats or telltale signs of trouble. My job required acute awareness of potential and emerging problems, so I was ever on the alert. When I used that mental orientation in the work of caring for Madeleine, I saw nothing but problems. Her failing health and limited ability to care for herself foreshadowed the prospect of her death.

We went through a few weeks of struggling. Then, one day, she said to me, "If you cannot be with me, it would be better if you were not trying to care for me." After we talked through the significance of what she meant, I realized that my mind was not at ease and my energy was constantly projecting into the future, where there was nothing but pain and loss. This emotional disturbance was affecting how I was in the present. In fact, I was hardly in the present moment at all.

I had to learn a new way of being. I needed to practice awareness of the present without letting my imagination jump forward into the future. I did not foresee how demanding it would be for me to be "presencing," which was the word I used to describe actively being in the present moment. If I was preparing Madeleine's lunch, my full attention had to be on that task. I needed to catch my mind as it wandered to what came after the present moment. But with practice, I became more adjusted to living in the now, and giving it my full attention. Little by little, things got easier.

As I adjusted my inner focus to the present, Madeleine let me know that she was aware of the change in me, and that she found me much easier to be around. For my part, I started to be in the present most of the time, and I connected to everyone and everything more fully. Eventually, I started to find it hard to think about the future at all, which was liberating. Instead of letting my thoughts create a fearful future, I was able to attend completely to whatever I was doing and whoever I was with.

During the remission period, and after I became her caregiver, Madeleine resumed painting in her studio, welcomed students to paint with her, and shared her spiritual view of the work. She would instruct each student, and note the progress they were making. With others, she simply conversed, since she believed that they were no longer in need of teaching.

But after only a year or so, she could no longer climb the stairs to her studio, and she stopped painting. I knew that it bothered her not to do what she loved doing. I could see that her strength was diminished, and I realized that her journey to the end of life was continuing.

The community care nursing team offered practical help. They accessed the Red Cross, who provided Madeleine with aids to make sitting more comfortable. They offered to bring in a hospital bed to be set up in the dining room, but she did not want that change. In the morning I would help her descend the stairs from our second-floor bedroom. She would sit in her favorite chair for her meals, and in the evening, she and I would navigate the stairs again so that she could sleep in her own bed. The community care nurses offered to come several times a week, but after the first few times, she asked them not to come, saying that I would provide for her needs.

During this time, the couple who were performing light therapy for Madeleine also began using energy in their healing work. Once, after a treatment, they asked if they could dowse our home for energy.

In their scan of the house, one of the practitioners used a long, flexible wire wand with a weight at the end, and the other used two L-shaped rods made of copper. They walked through the house separately, without either one working in the presence of the other, checking with their instruments. When they reconvened with me, the two investigators described what they found. Their instruments had both reacted to stimuli in exactly the same places in the house. They interpreted these reactions as geopathic energy emanating from the ground, deep beneath the house. Their research suggested that they had uncovered "geopathic stress zones,"[2] electromagnetic radiations that rise up through fault lines and are considered very

---

[2] For further information about geopathic stress see: http://geopathicstress.us/home

harmful to human health. People who have worked with geopathic energy have discovered a strong correlation between it and cancer.

My interest was raised and I did more research of my own, and found an epidemiological study conducted in Germany that strongly suggested that concentration of cancers coincides with the presence of geopathic fault lines. I also wanted to know if I could replicate the experience of the two energy healers.

I secured L-shaped copper rods and walked through my house by myself. I was surprised that my rods responded in the same place as the ones held by the investigators. Alarmingly, the energy showed up running through the side of the king-size bed that Madeleine slept on, but not on my side, and downstairs in the living room, the rods reacted to geopathic energy running through the chair where she sat to watch television.

I reached out to other dowsers and discovered that there was a general familiarity with this phenomenon, so I set about looking for ways to mitigate the effect of the geopathic energy. My healer friends recommended several methods for this, one of which worked completely.

I found that I had a facility with the rods. I began reading about dowsing, and practiced locating things with the rods. Through repeated practice, I developed a facility, achieving surprising results. While dowsing is most commonly associated with finding underground water, it is also regularly used to reveal buried pipes and oil tanks. I used my rods successfully to find lost jewelry and other items.

On one occasion, Madeleine asked if I could detect concentrations of negative energy. At the time, she had resumed teaching mandala painting, but she was seeing a smaller number of students. One evening, before retiring, she asked me if I thought the rods could detect a negative energy disturbance for her. I told her that I could only ask the rods if I could use them that way. She thought that perhaps someone's disturbed energy had stayed with her after a session. To my amazement, the rods responded in the affirmative. The rods can only be asked questions that can be answered with a simple yes or no, and in my experience, when they swung out, they were indicating a "yes" and when they moved into a crossing position, they indicated the answer was no.

When I asked if Madeleine had attracted negative energy, the rods moved into the open V position, indicating that the answer was yes. I then asked if I could clear the energy, and again the answer was positive. "How?" was my next question, but I could not ask a question that the rods could not answer via yes or no. When I explored some options for moving the energy, I got a strong positive from the rods, so I asked if the energy would clear with a Reiki blessing. Again, I got a positive answer. When I used the blessing I had learned from my Reiki teacher, the rods indicated that the negative energy had gone.

By this time, I had done considerable reading about the new cosmology. What I learned was that all of the energy that will ever be in the universe flared out all at once at the beginning of the universe. That energy is the source of all matter. What appears to our senses to be solid is, in reality, made up of fields of energy in the form of subatomic particles—atoms and molecules. We are made of the same energy that created the universe, and we are at the crest of a continuing evolutionary event. Moreover, we are surrounded by electromagnetic energy. Cell phones, radio and television, micro-waves and electric stoves, the wires that carry electricity into the buildings where we live and work are all carrying electromagnetism throughout our everyday lives. I should not have been surprised that simple copper rods would be sensitive to the impulses of energy. What amazed me at that time was that the energy was responding to specific questions. It seems that we exist in a sea of consciousness.

In a practical way, I am connecting to what the scientists have been telling us about the universe. My dowsing experience has been a union of the scientific and the spiritual. I am in touch with con-scious energy that responds to my questions, and I am using my mind to look for information. However it happens, through dows-ing I am drawing from the zero-point energy field, which scientists describe as the state that is a quantum memory that contains and records the entire experience of creation from the beginning into the future. Every human thought or word becomes part of that field, and goes into the shaping of the unfolding thrust of the universe.

In my research, I quickly discovered that few theologians have explored the connection between science and spirit. It may be that the deep fissure that has kept religion separate from science for cen-turies also keeps theologians from plumbing the new insights. On the other side, scientists are not expressing their insights into the cosmos in spiritual or meaningful terms. Perhaps they are worried about being ridiculed by their fellow scientists. To make matters worse, prominent atheists are expressing the opinion that, despite the evidence, there is no connection at all.

I am convinced that the more we understand the nature of the universe, especially the new cosmology, the more we can see more deeply into our spiritual yearnings. As authors like Thomas Berry note regarding the deep connections between the new cosmology and the mind's deepest aspirations, there is a healing of the breach. Seekers into the mystery are able to give voice to their quests. The upsurge of insights into the universe is fueling an expanding understanding of cosmology, and we can learn from it as metaphor for the truth at the heart of the cosmos.

My exploration of modern scientific findings about the universe is not focused on the mechanics of physics and astronomy. Rather, I see these breakthroughs in understanding as offering humanity more comprehensive knowledge about who and where we are in the story of the universe's unfolding. We are the generation with the potential to unite science and spirit into a new way of knowing. The primordial teacher about our place in nature is the cosmos.

Seeing how energy continually creates and unifies, simultaneously moving ahead and destroying, we can see the pulsating property of the substance of the universe. There is no new life that does not expire. I can examine that through the scientific metaphor or I can see the spiritual one, but both will take me deeper into the mystery of the single truth.

Madeleine and I knew that we were on the journey to the end of life itself. For her, the end was anticipated, and her spiritual work with the mandala had prepared her. I was the one who struggled to accept the end of her life's journey, but I was committed to accompany her, however long or short it would be. It turned out to be longer than either of us expected.

She often told me of a recurring dream/vision in which she saw herself walking down a dark corridor, but at the end of which there was an open door with bright light shining out. As she looked at the doorway, she saw her deceased mother standing within it, beckoning and welcoming her. Madeleine knew that she would be going through that door, and that love awaited her.

But as her mind prepared for death, her body rallied and did not go at the pace she would have liked. Months passed. The door vision dimmed, and Madeleine was saddened that she did not go through when she was ready. Her doctor, who saw her regularly at home, told her that her body was surprisingly strong and had a mind of its own.

In the days we had together, we resolved to communicate fully. There was no reason to leave anything unsaid, or to harbor regrets for not having told each other something important. Our conversations were very kind, and we each held each other with tenderness and compassion. Those days passed as though we were in a dream. There had been a lot of fighting in our earlier years, but the last period of our marriage was warm and gentle.

I had always thought of us as two trees in an orchard. We each had our sturdy trunk, rooted deeply in the Earth, and although our branches intertwined, we remained independent in our side-by-side connection. But during the years of our journey to Madeleine's death, there was a change. As she grew more dependent on my care, and could do less and less, not even bathe or dress herself, I found myself bursting with compassion. My heart cracked open, and I learned to love in a new way, and to give without expecting anything in return. There was no keeping mental accounts as I had done before. I simply met Madeleine in the moment, and did whatever was needed. I had found a new generosity, and a new willingness to be present to her. In return, Madeleine expressed her gratitude for even the smallest courtesies. As Shakespeare wrote in *Romeo and Juliet,* "The more I give to thee, the more I have, for both are infinite."

My heart ached, both from seeing her deteriorate and knowing that she would be passing through the membrane that separated the living from the dead. She asked me to use the dowsing rods to inquire about her sense of having visitors from the spirit world. I was in for another surprise. In the years of being without religion, I had been prepared to accept that when you die, your energy returns to the stream. Now I was being asked to use the rods to investigate the presence of particular individuals we knew who had died, years ago in some cases. What I found was a consistent and varied presence of people connected by bonds of family, love, and a lasting commitment to one another.

Whenever I asked about Madeleine's mother, the dowsing rods reported that she was present. Her mother seemed to always be with her. On the other hand, whenever I asked about her father, he was rarely there. Other family members came and went. Madeleine's sister Mary was present often, and her younger brother Louis also visited frequently. Other members of her family or deceased friends came along as well. Madeleine often wondered aloud whether any of the spirits that surrounded her had messages for her. Mostly the answer was that they were there to support her and keep her company. She never asked about their world, and was content with whatever answers came through the rods.

When the end came, it came quickly. Strength left Madeleine's body one night as we were going upstairs together. I called the doctor, and he arranged for the palliative care team from Victoria's hospice organization to make an emergency call to our house. With impressive efficiency and care, they made Madeleine comfortable and gave her sedatives for her pain. The doctor came a few hours later and gave the nurses directions for the drug levels, and by morning Madeleine was dead.

I discovered her at about 3:00 a.m. The emergency nurse from hospice pronounced her dead, and removed the kit they had brought to see to her needs. Alone with my wife of thirty-six years, I was overcome. I knelt by her body and cried until the sun came up. In first light of dawn, when I saw her face, I was overwhelmed by the peace that had returned to her. Her beauty in death was radiant. All of the suffering that had been etched on her face from years of contending with the disease were erased. She was translucent.

As I looked at her in the light of dawn, I recalled what I had heard in a workshop about death and grieving. The former chaplain who ran the workshop said that ancient cultures believed that the spirit stayed with the body for a period after physical death. Entertaining that thought, I picked up the dowsing rods and asked if I could be in contact with Madeleine's spirit. The rods swung into the affirmative position. I asked if she was with her mother and her sister. The rods indicated no. I was surprised. Asking a different way, I inquired if she was now with her guardian spirit. Again, no. I then asked if she was still here in the room with me. This time the rods swung vigorously to the yes position.

I was engulfed by the event's sacredness. I got a basin of warm water and washed her body. Knowing there was more I could do to extend the sacred moment, I began to anoint her, starting with her face and head, and slowly applying the oil to every area of her body.

After I completed this ritual, I was depleted. I went downstairs and made a pot of tea. When I came back to the bedroom with my tea, I sensed that there was a different energy in the room, and that her spirit was no longer there.

I used the dowsing rods again to ask if I could be in contact with Madeleine. The rods swung to the yes position. I said that if I was communicating with Madeleine, I needed a sign. The rod in my left hand swung smartly around and pointed to my heart. That had never happened before, and I needed no other proof. I asked her if she was still in the room with her body, and the answer was no. I asked her if she was at peace. Yes. Was she with her guardian spirit? Yes. Was she with her mother and her sister and brother? Yes. Then I asked her a question that seemed to come out of nowhere: "Are you in time?" The rods said no. "Are you in some place?" Again, no. "Are you conscious?" Yes. "Will you always be able to communicate with me?" Yes. "And will I be able to communicate with you?" Yes.

I have been able to make contact with Madeleine's energy in the years since that extraordinary moment. Every time, I have been satisfied that I am having a two-way communication. I have no doubt that the energy that was personalized in bodily form is still intact and conscious. What is beyond doubt for me is that Madeleine's spirit is in the universe and is able to interact with me.

I have no doubt that I communicate with the energy body of the person I knew and loved on Earth. There is two-way communication. Madeleine's once incarnated energy abides intact, and this has made me change my mind about personal survival beyond the membrane we call death.

In addition to the peace I feel about having a continuing connection to all of my deceased loved ones, this experience confirmed the substance of my new understanding of the universe. On a very personal level, the new cosmology was affirmed for me. The basis of spirituality is the universe, and that is critically important to understand.

8

My Return to Life

*Today, something is happening to the whole structure of
human consciousness. A fresh kind of life is starting. Driven
by the forces of love, the fragments of the world are seeking
each other, so that the world may come into being.*
—Pierre Teilhard de Chardin

MADELEINE WAS GONE. After five years of intense caregiving, I was alone with memories and grief, surrounded
by her absence. The house was empty. The pain was intense, and I
could not assimilate it for quite a while.

For most of my working life, my world had been defined by
service. Cancer had reshaped Madeleine's independence, and my
own. Her illness had made us interdependent in a new way, with
each of us looking to the other. Although, at the beginning of my
caregiving, I would not have bet on my ability to stay committed
to a long-term role as attendant, my choice came down to making the decision anew each day. I chose to meet Madeleine's needs,
cook and serve appetizing meals, look after all the small things, and

attend to the reality of daily living. The circumference of my attention had grown small indeed. As she drew closer to the threshold between life and death, I neared that portal with her. Even though I knew that she was walking that path alone, I traveled in lockstep with her; by fully attending to her in each moment, I moved in sync with her. When Madeleine died, being alive seemed strange. Not only was my partner gone, but my purpose was ripped away once again, and I felt intensely alone.

I had the feeling that I was falling into an abyss. I'd had a similar feeling after leaving the priesthood, but this was more intense. After spending years accompanying Madeleine to the end of her life, my heart cracked open. I knew I had learned to love in a new way: more completely, less self-interested, purer in spirit. Madeleine's loss was more intense than any other feeling I had ever known.

There were practical things to do, to keep me busy. I placed an obituary in the newspaper and notified key people, asking them to tell others that Madeleine had died. I arranged for the Memorial Society to have her body cremated, and I planned a memorial service, which took place three weeks after her death. I decided to preside at the service, and chose the music and asked people to speak about her. The service was held in Victoria at the John T. Shields Building, the union's building which had been named in my honor. The auditorium was filled to capacity, and the gathering included our dearest friends from Texas, Madeleine's mandala-painting students, people from the community, and Madeleine's family from Toronto. I also invited family members and close friends to a dinner afterward, so we could continue to talk about Madeleine and celebrate her life.

In the immediate aftermath of her death, I could not engage in anything. I could not even attend the spirituality circle that I facilitated, much less take on my role at Leadership Victoria. I was anchored in the vortex of a black hole of grief.

Finally, after months of intense grieving, I was ready for some kind of activity, and I set about turning my house into a museum of Madeleine's art. Seventeen large mandalas were the legacy of her years of work. Each piece took her about a year to paint, and provided a symbolic map of her life and a picture of her innermost being. I framed all of the paintings and hung them throughout the house until every available wall space held one of her mandalas.

Years before, a group of Tibetan Buddhist monks had come to Victoria to construct a mandala from grains of colored sand. The monks painstakingly added a single grain of sand at a time for weeks until the mandala was complete. During the making of the mandala, the Dalai Lama visited the Art Gallery of Greater Victoria, and at a public reception, he thanked Madeleine for the use of her mandalas to publicize the event.

Once the exquisitely beautiful mandala had been completed, the monks swept up the sand and poured it into the sea in a demonstration of nonattachment. Their act was a reminder of the impermanence of all things, which is one of the tenets of Buddhism. Not only did the monks make no effort to preserve their work of art, but they consciously destroyed it. The occasion had greatly influenced Madeleine and she wanted to follow in that tradition, so she had asked me to give away many of her mandalas. My next task was to put my energy into distributing the paintings according to her wishes.

In the months that followed, as I continued to focus on Madeleine, her wishes, and her estate, I realized how easy it would be for me to continue to live in the anteroom to death. But when spring arrived with new life all around me—cherry blossoms and daffodils—I could not help but notice that the universe was renewing itself. As I walked through Victoria's beautiful gardens, I realized I had a choice. I could ignore the impulse of the cycle of the seasons and stay focused on mourning Madeleine's death, or I could choose to come back to life with the rest of nature. But I did not know how to do that.

My habit of staying in the present moment had subsumed my previous orientation to the future. I did not want to go back to the way I had been—as the head of the union, constantly recalculating my life to meet future goals. How could I rejoin the world? I sat in my garden and meditated on that question.

The answer that came to me was profound. I could say yes to the universe. I had already developed the conviction that I am in this world to contribute to the universe's unfolding, to be part of the intricate cosmic pattern, so I resolved to affirm whatever the universe presented me.

The first thing to happen after I made this decision was that I received a call from the program director at Leadership Victoria, where I was the chairman of the board, responsible for the delivery of community based training for volunteer leadership. The program director had been on a waiting list to have extensive surgery in Montreal, and she had just heard from her doctor that she had a date for the operation.

The Leadership Victoria class met as a group once a month for a community learning day, and each meeting had a committee responsible for organizing and conducting the event. There were also group projects that teams of the participants planned and carried out. Someone had to carry the reins until the program director returned, which she estimated to be about six weeks. I said, yes, I would step in while the program director took medical leave, and make sure the program continued.

Six weeks turned into six months. I went to work downtown every day, and coordinated Leadership Victoria. At first, I felt rusty. I had not administered an organization since I had stepped down as president of the British Columbia Government and Service Employees Union, but I quickly found that it was a relatively straightforward role being the project director for the various facets of the organization. Suddenly, I was very busy and feeling challenged again.

One day, Sally, one of the volunteers, whom I had known since my days at Victoria Family and Children's Services, called me and suggested that I recruit a friend of hers to become a volunteer on the curriculum committee. Sally gave me a description of the woman she had in mind: Robin June Hood held a Ph.D. from the University of Victoria in curriculum development, had done international development and peace work in Latin America, and was currently doing contract work focusing on indigenous education. This prospective volunteer sounded perfect for Leadership Victoria. Moreover, she was doing some work for a nongovernmental organization whose office was in the same building as my own. I resolved to get in touch.

After a few abortive attempts to meet up, I dropped into the

143

office and invited Robin to lunch. We felt comfortable right away, and before we had even ordered lunch, we were in deep and engaging conversation. On so many levels, I connected warmly with Robin, and our lunch extended over two hours. She was beautiful, interesting, and charming, and she had spent much of her life working for social justice, as had I. By the end of our lunch, my interest had shifted from organizational to personal, and I I wanted to get to know this woman better.

The chance came the following week. Sally, who had suggested that I meet Robin, was organizing a fundraiser for another local charity. She was selling tickets, and when I agreed to buy one, she mentioned that Robin had also bought a ticket to the event. I immediately called Robin and invited her to go with me to Sally's event, and she readily agreed.

But now I found myself in an awkward position. I had not dated anyone since I was a teenager, since Madeleine and I had begun our relationship as working partners. Close, creative engagement in the context of our mutual work for the Church had drawn us together, but we had repressed any open expression of physical attraction to each other for the four years we worked together. Though our friendship eventually turned to love, sexuality was not the foundation of our relationship. In any new partner, I wanted a balance of love, mutual interests, emotional compatibility, and a healthy sex life.

My marriage to Madeleine had been based on mutual respect and love from the beginning, but it did not include much physical intimacy. Eventually, as part of the resolution to this dilemma, Madeleine had given me her blessing to have sexual relations with other women. Through the thirty-six years of our marriage, I had been sexually attracted to other women, but I was never promiscuous. In fact, I had not been inclined to take advantage of all of the sexual opportunities that came my way.

I also realized I was a complicated individual who had started my life as a priest, committed to celibacy. I needed to work through the hang-ups that came from more than a decade of trying to avoid gossip and public scandal, which was something I had always feared. My sense of decency and my wish to protect my reputation were always in play.

For my fourteen years as union president, I had lived alone during the week in an apartment near my office. There, I had a love affair with a woman who was sensitive to my circumstances. I was in a high-profile position and aware of the attendant risk of negative publicity that would have resulted from any scandal, but she was discrete and protective of my reputation.

This woman cared deeply for me, and had loved me for many years. She wanted a normal relationship, but I was not free and did not want to lead her on. While I was in a sexless marriage, it was a marriage that I was committed to, so I constrained myself from publicly dating anyone. I never felt free.

At this stage of my grieving, I was not looking for a new relationship, in part because I was unsure whether I would be a good candidate for one at that point. Because I was giving expression to all of the intense feelings as they arose, my emotional energy was spent, but I was still periodically gripped by feelings of loss. Deep, heartrending anguish would wash over me, unbidden and unexpected. Although I was near the end of the intense grief, the loss of Madeleine still affected me. With Robin, I was venturing into unknown territory.

The Victoria Hospice program at the hospital had a counseling service for people affected by the death of a loved one. I had been seeing a therapist since Madeleine's death, and he was aware of the state of my heart, so I sought his wisdom as a sounding board. I wondered whether falling in love during the grieving process would nullify the love or diminish the grief. What he advised me was that I was not betraying the departed loved one by experiencing the joy of new love. I would always remember Madeleine. I confided in my therapist that I had contacted her with the rods to ask if I was offending her by opening my heart to someone new. The answer through the rods was no, and she had blessed my joy of finding someone to love fully. My therapist told me that life always seeks a way to embrace love, and that I was a most fortunate man to find true love at any time in life.

Fortunate! I was indeed privileged to find someone who loved me wholly and fully. Robin came into my orbit when I said yes to the universe, and we continue to be conscious of the gift in both our lives

I am older than Robin by fifteen years. The difference in age was a question for Robin, but it did no turn out to be an obstacle. Though I would continue to grow older, I would not necessarily become aged in the process. In my experience, our relationship invigorates me, keeps my interests current, and prompts me to find ways to continue the contribution I enjoy making to the world. Being receptive to Robin's energy and interests, I am renewed, and my *response-ability* increases.

My sweet relationship with Robin brought me another delight-ful surprise in giving me the chance to experience fatherhood. At the beginning of our relationship, Robin's daughter, Nicola Angelique, was nineteen years old and attending university at McGill in Montreal. When Nikki came home for summer at the end of the semester, she was highly curious about the man who was in love with her mom. Robin had warned me that, in the past, Nikki had been hostile to men who were courting her, considering them unworthy of her. But by the end of the summer, Nikki had captured my heart with her generosity and openness. To my delight, she was open to a relationship with me that allows us to relate as father and daughter. She continues to grow into an unusually intel-ligent and vibrant young woman, with interests that take her deeply into the ecological movement and link her passion for aboriginal justice.

Robin raised Nikki on her own, without the father's involvement. Since I have never had children, I am happy that Nikki welcomes me as a paternal influence in her life. I feel singularly blessed to be met in my love for her, and for her including me in her life as a father figure. Her love is one of the most delicious gifts of a gener-ous universe.

I have found that by saying yes to the stream of events that the universe has sent my way, my life overflowed with abundance. I have taken jobs that have been interesting and rewarding. After marrying, Robin and I moved to a breathtaking home on a Gulf Island while I served as executive director at an educational cen-ter and then began teaching at Vancouver Island University (VIU). When I took up a fellowship at the University of Victoria's Centre for the Study of Religion and Society, we moved back to our home in Victoria, and I continued to teach at VIU as well as volunteered as the head of the Centre for Earth and Spirit.

Since I said yes to the universe, my life has been enriched with new friends, a flow of income that keeps us well, and an expanding opportunity to deepen and expand. I could not have designed a better path than the one that opened after I responded positively to the opening doors as well as the closing ones. Sometimes the greatest insights and benefit in my life arose from the things I stumbled over and the pain that ensued. Those missteps created as much learning and benefit as the things that went well.

My journey from religion to spirituality was not a straight line. Nonetheless, there were some clear steps along the way. I began with a commission from my grandfather that I would play a role of religious leader: "the first American Pope." My family was religious, and I was raised with a strong sense of the divine presence. I went from home to the seminary to train to become a priest. I grew closer to the sacred, participating in the symbolic sacramental rituals of the ancient Roman Catholic Church.

However, in the seminary I also learned how modern science had uncovered new information about the Bible, which is the foundation of both Judaism and Christianity. This new revelation severely undermined many of the suppositions that formed the basis of Christian belief. The universe was providing an opportunity to renew and reform many of the outmoded expressions of religion. Spirit offered religion an excellent opportunity "to say yes." A strong new consciousness was impelling the Church to acknowledge contemporary revelation. But the Church broke faith with that call, and in that betrayal, I lost faith in the Church.

When I left the Church, I had to step blindly back into the secular, and took on the world's many demands in order to survive the rough-and-tumble of modern life. One of the requirements of this reentry was sexuality, which I did not handle very well. I did much better with work. Doing social work, counseling people, and supervising new workers came easily to me. I said yes to union work, learned to be a warrior defending the rights of others, and rose to the demands of leadership. I learned the art of politics and stood up on behalf of public services. In pursuing the hero's journey, I was given the gift of a vision. I came to understand the mythic and how it was operating in me. One of the biggest steps on my way to spirituality was the recognition that the inner world creates the outer, and that there is energy in the synchronization of the two.

Discovery of the mythic in my psyche opened the door to the wonders of the universe as it is revealing itself. This transformative insight was the most impacting discovery on my journey. Cosmology's profound, recent breakthroughs are providing humanity with an entirely new set of concepts that reunites consciousness, spirit, and matter—and allowed me to discover spirit in the universe, reorienting my thinking.

Discovering cosmology took me strongly back to Earth. In nature, I came into harmony with the flow of creative energy. The environment is the universe made immediate. We come from it, and we are relearning to hold it sacred. Along with a renewed appreciation of the wild and unspoiled, I have developed a new respect for the First Nations of the world. They live in harmony with nature and prosper in that relationship.

My spirituality journey took another dimension as I learned to be a caregiver for Madeleine on her journey to the end of her life. The opportunity to deepen my sense of living in the present moment came from the gift of being with someone who knew they were dying and needed to live intensively in the present. The uncounted benefits of living in love and service without strings flowed to me during that six-year period.

During much of the time I was being a caregiver, I facilitated a group for men seeking to develop spirituality in their lives. On a weekly basis, the group came together and shared at a profound level of trust and openness. In the energy of that circle, I came into direct contact with spiritual energy.

At heart, the understanding that I am an integral element of the conscious, living universe has reshaped my orientation to the universal realm. An unbroken chain of being connects me to the beginning. The unity of the cosmos connects me to all. The unfolding nature of time and space puts me at the leading edge of cosmic evolution. There is purpose in everything I do and say. I am part of the blossoming of consciousness. I am a part of the All.

9

Dancing on the Cutting Edge

You must live in the present, launch yourself on every wave,
find your eternity in each moment.
—Henry David Thoreau

THE INTERNAL DYNAMIC of the unfolding universe is so unified that everything that it manifests is part of the oneness.
We are just becoming aware that consciousness and spirit are its
characteristics from the very first energy impulse. The universe that
is generating itself embraces everything in its unity.

Swimme and Berry assert that from the moment of the great
flaring forth, the universe develops in such a way that each event is
woven into the fabric of every other. They say that protons may be
thought of as being in a place but that they are also just as legitimately present to all the particles with which they have ever inter-
acted. Unity of time and place puts everything into a single web of
connection. "No part of the present can be isolated from any other

part of the present or the past or the future."[1] This was a strange and wonderful notion. I was excited to think that I might finally have found the key I was looking for.

My excitement grew as I began to digest what the quantum physicist David Bohm added to this proposition. He concluded that all matter in the universe is interconnected by quantum waves, and referred to "an overwhelming sense of 'unbroken wholeness' in the world."[2]

Because there is a continuity of everything in the universe, the evolutionary process has produced a seamless unfolding from the beginning of the emergence of time. The energy that has generated that blossoming of the cosmos is conscious and spirit filled. Each person who has evolved from the primordial dynamic is connected and stays connected to the continuous creative flow.

Another force in the evolution of the universe is attraction. Swimme calls this force "allurement." Gravity is a manifestation of the universe's power of attraction. From the smallest protons to the swirling galaxies, attraction creates the shape of the cosmos. In the context of human presence on Earth, allurement can be seen as love.

In a conscious universe, love is a binding, uniting force. I feel it in nature when I watch an eagle soar or a whale passing. I know that the love that is stirred in me is an attracting force. Love of the animals in my life is something I experience at a different level.

[1] Brian Swimme and Thomas Berry, *The Universe Story: From the Primordial Flaring Forth to the Ecozoic Era—A Celebration of the Unfolding of the Cosmos,* San Francisco, CA: HarperCollins, 1992, p. 29.
[2] McTaggart, Lynne, *The Field: Quest for the Secret Force of the Universe.* New York, NY: HarperCollins, 2002.

These creatures that so openly give love and devotion activate a deep bond.

Love has long been the song of poets and artists. I have been blessed by an abundance of love in my life. My parents and grandparents, extended family, and circle of friends—all people I have loved—have taught me to open my heart. The women who have connected with me with tenderness have invited me to venture more deeply into love, and evoked change throughout my life. Pain and sorrow combine with deep passion and openheartedness to generate a well of love to transform.

As I call to mind the people in my life who I have loved and who are now dead, I see that the bond of love is still strong and active. Death has not diminished my feelings of tenderness and connection. I think of them and experience their presence. Consciousness crosses the divide between this life and the ongoing flow of time.

Because I am interested in how human beings, as points of energy individuated in time, persist in the universe beyond death, I began looking at traditional wisdom. Every tradition and culture has had some sense of an abiding presence of human spirit, and each one's way of speaking about the ongoing individual consciousness is unique, yet in many ways similar.

The sense of continuity beyond death is ancient. Chi or qi, spirit, soul, prana, and kundalini are all terms that the world's religious traditions and many First Nations' mythologies speak about the life force, which continues after death. Each tradition draws upon its people's understanding of the universe to put language to their intuition about an afterlife.

All the traditional ways of thinking and all of the new insights are united within the concept of cosmic energy. Each religious tradition, along with each new scientific discovery, sees the universe as a single unified actor, conscious and alive, spiritual and loving. Everything that exists comes out of the single, integrated whole that both contains and preserves everything there is within itself—an insight that I found consistent with my dowsing experiences.

My experiences of being able to communicate with loved ones who have gone through the membrane that encloses this life has convinced me that the state of awareness is not dependent on physical form. The energy that is at once past, present, and future carries consciousness and spirit, and bridges the condition of this life and the state we call death.

American biologist Bruce Lipton discovered that there is awareness at the cellular level. Deep emotions such as fear or love send a cascade of chemicals to the cells, and the entire organism responds with a high level of communication, triggering responses that vary depending on the environment in each cell.[3]

Likewise, Thomas Berry has no difficulty saying that the universe is sentient. Berry observes that empirical inquiry into the universe has shown that "from its beginning in the galactic system to its earthly expression in human consciousness, the universe carries within itself a psychic-spiritual as well as a physical-material dimension." Otherwise, Berry reasons, consciousness would emerge "out of nowhere." He goes on to say humanity "activates

---

[3] Bruce Lipton, *The Biology of Belief: Unleashing the Power of Consciousness, Matter and Miracles,* New York, NY: Hay House, Inc., 2005.

the most profound dimension of the universe itself, its capacity to reflect on and celebrate itself in conscious self-awareness."

Discerning the Cutting Edge

The metaphor that best describes my place in the universe is a surfer riding in the curl of a perfect wave. I am the surfer who becomes one with the energy of the wave. I ride its breaking edge and surf along its leading edge with serenity.

This metaphor is inspired by the new knowledge we have acquired about the universe. Since NASA captured the graphic images of the Cosmic Background Radiation with its COBE probe in the early 1990s, the scientific community has come to near unanimity in developing a picture of the beginning of the cosmos.

In the beginning, originating power brought forth the universe from a state of pure potential. The incipient universe burst forth in an intense flaring of heat, light, and power. As Swimme and Berry describe it, "All the energy that would ever exist in the entire course of time erupted as a single quantum—a singular gift—existence. If in the future, stars would blaze and lizards would blink in their light, these actions would be powered by the same numinous energy that flared forth at the dawn of time."[4]

I find it impossible to visualize adequately the quantum of energy either at the beginning or now, almost fourteen billion years later. I imagine at the beginning that when the universe erupted

---

[4] Swimme and Berry, op.cit. p17.

into being, a small, intense, incredibly hot ball of conscious ener-gy—a soup of swirling particles and atoms that seethed with power. Because space/time expands as a single dimension, when the uni-verse was only moments old (time), the space that the energy quan-tum existed within was relatively tiny. (I realize, however, that when I picture the ball in my mind's eye, I am in the trap of visualizing the universe as a thing outside of me. In reality, everything that will ultimately be created by the energy is only potential within the emerging whole.)

At the beginning, from the field of pure possibility, particles emerged from the density of compacted energy. With unimagin-ably great heat, light flowed forth into the void, creating time and space as it expanded. The beginning is not an event in time. The originating power does not exist in time or space. Time and space begin with the flaring forth. The universe is a coherent whole of which time and space are essential constituents.

Now, an estimated 13.7 billion years after the universe's initial flaring, we find ourselves on Earth, orbiting a star in a side arm of the Milky Way, one of hundreds of billions of galaxies that have emerged. Over the past few decades, we have discovered a massive amount of information about the beginning and the nature of our universe. What do we know about the present?

Einstein concluded that time and space, which we experience as two dimensions, are aspects of a single phenomenon. In the scientific world, this is referred to as space/time. Contemporary cosmologists conclude that the characteristics of space/time were determined by the universe in the tiniest fraction of a second after the great flaring. The strength of the gravitational force and the electromagnetic field along with the two nuclear interactions would govern the nature of the cosmic activity within the overriding unity. These relationships, adopted by the universe right at the beginning, would determine how fast the universe would expand and the nature of all of its subsequent relationships. Had there been the tiniest variation in either direction, the universe could not have developed at all.

In the energy of the initial flaring of the universe, the searing heat created the first elements, which in turn combined and caused the energy field to expand. The symmetry of the fundamental architecture of the cosmos began to shape the future. The density fluctuations of the earliest stages were imprinted on the unfolding, giving eventual shape to the formation of galactic structures. As the expansion cooled, the wild creation and annihilation of elements that characterized the earliest stages ceased, and the coherence took on an elegant form.

Cosmologists have looked at the expansion of the energy and observed that, over time, the energy cooled and its outward thrust generated quantum fluctuations or ripples. The gas clouds containing the primal elements were ignited, flaring into galaxies and stars.

In the process of the outward direction of the early universe, the expansion of gases and the electromagnetic energy field set not just one galaxy into existence but created hundreds of billions of galaxies. Some scientists calculate that there could easily be five hundred billion galaxies in existence, with each one containing hundreds of billions of stars, too many to count.

With the Hubble telescope, science began peering back into the origin of the earliest galactic formation. Using the speed of light as a measure, Hubble scientists were able to determine the age of the universe. The universe is not five thousand years old as was assumed a mere hundred years ago. The estimated age of the universe—13.7 billion years—comes from the calculation of the time it would take light, traveling at 300,000 kilometers per second, to reach Earth. The refurbished Hubble satellite has captured images from when the universe was much younger—between six hundred million to eight hundred million years old.[5]

NASA is responsible for another less well-known spacecraft that is measuring changes in heat within the universe since the time of the Big Bang. Following the Cosmic Background Explorer's (COBE) measurement of the cosmic background radiation, NASA launched the Wilkinson Microwave Anisotropy Probe (WMAP) in 2001. The intent was to measure the cosmic background radiation radiant heat across the full sky. As the highest-precision instrument ever devoted to the exploration of the universe, WMAP is responsible for depicting the expansion of the universe in space and time, from the beginning to the present.[6] WMAP's map-like diagram shows the expansion of space/time, and how the universe has developed.

[5] Peter N. Spotts. "Hubble telescope glimpses universe's earliest galaxies." The *Christian Science Monitor*, January 5, 2010.
[6] National Aeronautics and Space Administration, Wilkinson Microwave Anisotropy Probe. <http://map.gsfc.nasa.gov/>

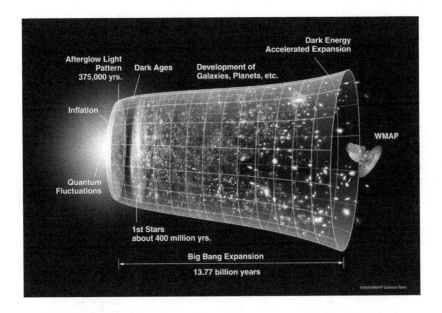

Figure 1. WMAP's History of Universe

The shape of the cosmos surprised me. The expanse is not circular like the ancients thought. WMAP shows that the development of the universe has expanded in linear shape, but is not infinite. The thrust of the early expansion, called the inflation phase, pushed space/time outward, largely determining space/time's subsequent linear shape. Over the ensuing millennia, the expanse of the universe matched its extension in time. WMAP also demonstrates that the development of the cosmos along the time axis is comparable to its growth in space.

As Einstein predicted, time and space flow in a linear direction, and WMAP shows that the universe experienced its greatest growth at the very beginning of time. Time travel into the future seems only to be possible in the imagination. Likewise, the ancient image of a cyclical universe in which time rotates with the heavens, an eternal past, is not supported by WMAP's discoveries. The belief in the mandala of time, in which history is continually repeated, has been supplanted by the discoveries of science.

Cosmologists point out that the universe is an ongoing energy event, and the WMAP image confirms the unity of the expansion. The entire history of the universe is not lost. It becomes present in this moment. The continuing unfolding of the cosmos, taking place in time, produces the now.

The expansion from the nucleus of the Big Bang occurred in direct proportion to the duration. The space of the universe is finite, and can be grasped as a multivalent "here." Importantly, WMAP demonstrates that there is no future beyond the present moment. The frame in which the data was collected contains both the past and the present, but nothing beyond the now. This highly sophisticated analysis of the microwave heat in the universe proves that there is no time beyond now and no space outside the universe. Everything, therefore, is happening right now, in this moment, at the edge of the expanding cosmos. We are on the cutting edge of space and time.

I am excited by the idea that we are in the moment at which the entire universe is unfolding. The universe has created this moment and this place. It has been developing for almost fourteen billion years to bring this moment into being. The entire evolutionary history of the Earth has happened for this moment. Everything that the universe has experienced continues into this moment. In the cosmos, where no energy is lost and none can be added, we are the focal point of the unfolding. All of the energy that has produced the visible universe is present all around us at this moment. What we do with the energy we have determines the nature of the continuing moment.

The way the cosmos has evolved—through tumult and chaos, attraction and symmetry, choice and chance—shows the amazing diversity and direction that the universe has chosen. What is in the now is the only thing that can be. As far as we know, there are no alternative universes, and of all the scenarios that might have existed, no other scenarios actually do exist in this moment. Because the universe has created this moment as its culmination, all other possibilities vanish once this moment comes into being. In this moment, we are that which is. We find the groove and align ourselves with the direction that 13.7 billion years of evolution has brought about.

The universe has chosen this moment to reveal the knowledge that can make a shift in its unfolding. Each sentient being also manifests in the present, and is aligned to the unfolding. According to quantum theory, there is choice at every level of being. As humans, we must consciously choose to be in the moment and accept whatever is. Our choices are shaping this moment and the next.

Our freedom also allows us not to choose to be present in the moment, and to resist what is. By resisting alignment, however, we create stress for ourselves and static in our energy field. On the other hand, when we go with the energy, there is a peace and a harmony which we experience as *flow*. We actively contribute to the dynamics that are producing the next moment. When we come into sync with what is, we are like water in a deep river. Rather than be in control of this flow, we are in it and of it, part of the entire cosmos at the leading edge of the space/time.

I have a reverence for all that goes into this moment. The more I am able to appreciate the universe's complexity and its simplicity, the more I sense the sacred. The majesty and mystery of how this moment comes about overwhelms my capacity to take things for granted. The sheer creative confluence that brings us into time at this moment is impossible to apprehend fully. There is no doubt in my mind, however, that we are here for a purpose. Since each person, each sentient being is unique, our contributions to the unfolding of the cosmos are also unique.

Every one of us is an energy center, reflecting the universe. Like everything else in our cosmos, we are more energy than matter. The energy that animates us is the energy that has given rise to the entire universe. Through the presence of the human in history, the universe has added an evolving consciousness. In the context of our cosmic mission, we are truly participating in the ongoing creation of the emerging universe.

We live at a moment when the mass of evidence gives humanity the ability to surpass the flawed materialistic worldview that often shackles the human imagination. If we understand that the nature of our participation with the universe is co-creative, we see the divine mystery in our activity. We are of the universe; channeling the energy of the creative fire; emerging in the consciousness of the entire cosmos, revealing the divine. We are matter and spirit in a single form. As such, we allow the divine to show forth another dimension of the sacred in the wonder of this moment.

I am optimistic that the new revelations about the universe

will produce deep transformation in our social order. Our new thinking about the universe as acting, sentient, and self-determining its future is so unlike the older visions that, in short order, humanity will begin to see the entire world differently.

The new and growing perspective offers the human race a fresh way to understand our collective place on Earth. We are coming to appreciate that we descend from the Earth's long evolutionary history, and we are seeing our place in the universe as children of our star, the sun. The sun gives us energy, climate, food, and the entire context of our lives. Humanity is the product of eons of evolution, and is integral to the continuing evolutionary history of the cosmos. I see us in the wave curl of space/time. The universe is not here for us; rather, we are of and for the universe.

We humans have the capacity to love and feel compassion for others and ourselves, and we have intelligence and consciousness that enables us to understand what is happening and assess its significance. We might act very differently toward the Earth and its creatures if we fully understood that we are the very stuff of this planet, far more than visitors on a heavenly journey. A change of perspective about what we are meant to be in the wave curl of time could revolutionize our approach to everything. Rather than viewing the Earth as a basket of goods for our use, we might visualize ourselves as participants in a dynamic community of beings, each with a role and purpose in the diversity of life on Earth. Rather than allowing—or even causing—the destruction of countless numbers of species every day, we might begin respecting and protecting our fellow members of the Earth community. In addition, we have a collective responsibility for the entire human family. The emerging awareness among humankind is that we need to form a circle of care for one another, including humans and more-than-humans.

The gift of the universe in our time is revelation of the singleness and interconnectedness of everything. An abundance of insight is pouring into our awareness that we are creatures of nature. Before it is too late, humanity has the opportunity to reverse out destructive behaviors and begin to preserve the natural world. We know that we have a choice. We can devastate what remains of nature, or we can elect to preserve it in an unspoiled state for the future of the Earth. We need to take to heart Einstein's wisdom: In order to solve the problems we face, we need a different level of thinking than we had when we created them. Where is this new thinking going to come from? I believe that the universe is actively showing us a new way.

In the face of the outpouring of new cosmological workings of the Earth and the universe, I have a growing sense of time speeding up. Perhaps it is an increasing sense of the crisis the Earth is in, or perhaps it is the universe preparing for another rapid expansion of space/time. With the insight that now is a crucial moment in the unfolding, we have a corresponding responsibility to stay in the curl of energy that is moving us ahead.

The new future at the breaking edge of time has to be about more than stopping the harm and damage. While stopping the degradation of the planet is essential, the universe has more in mind than that. The entire cosmos is poised on the brink of expansion. How it expands depends on the culmination of all that has happened in the past, plus what happens in this moment. The range of impulses by all of humanity is constantly impacting the direction of space/ time.

In a dance, we feel the rhythm and the tempo of the music, discern the flow of the energy in our bodies, and come into resonance with the harmonics. Dancers feel the energy and respond on an instinctive level. Attunement is something that indicates that we have come into synchronization with the tempo of the events of the moment. I feel that harmony in nature. By the sea, in the mountains, or in the woods, the energy of the surrounding environment brings me into coherence. In cities, I am often more conscious of the massed talent and ingeniousness of humanity as people strive to create a humanized environment. At times, however, I feel that we are out of coherence with the natural harmonies, and I have to refocus my intention to be in harmony with the Earth by meditating or practicing conscious unity with all being.

Bringing positive emotions into my consciousness shifts my inner presence. I have learned that having a loving attitude is one way to enhance the influence of my human contribution to the universe. When angry, chaotic and negative emotions radiate out from my heart, they negatively impact everyone around me, leaving my environment worse off for my presence.

Almost all the creatures in the Earth community instinctively contribute to the wellbeing of the planet simply by being themselves. Nature has attuned each creature to fulfill its highest purpose within the world's interconnected network. Only humans have the highly developed ability to exercise free choice that can lead to our capacity to do things that are not good for the planet and its inhabitants. A higher onus rests on the human to consciously align with the energies of the planet. This is why, in this time of global crisis, humanity has the responsibility to change the way we have been conducting ourselves on Earth.

The insight about the horizon of time raises the imperative of acting now. The universe does not guarantee a future. When we attempt to foretell the future, quantum theory points to the probability that space/time will continue to unfold, just as we perceive them to have done in the past, but there is no guarantee. There is only now.

Our discovery about the nature of the expansion of space/time should convince us that we only have this continuing moment to alter our thinking and our behavior. Future generations will have every right to ask us, "What did you do in the time of the world's crisis to save the planet?"

Afterword

By Briony Penn, Ph.D.

Although John didn't include a last chapter of his personal story, it begs telling as it speaks volumes about the interconnectedness of the cosmos.

Just before John met his second wife, Robin, my closest friend, she underwent heart surgery. She was worn out by her long years as an activist and filmmaker for the peace movement in Central America and the environmental movement in British Columbia. The years of battling for people with no voices, who were enduring severe conditions and violence as they squared up against the corporate powers had left Robin's heart damaged. It had also been broken by a long and difficult relationship with a revolutionary priest from El Salvador with whom she had a daughter, Nikki. For the first ten years of Nikki's life, Robin traveled with her in and out of a war-torn country, helping import medicine and export films to raise awareness of the war and its causes. Robin tried to convince Nikki's father to move to the safety of Canada and raise Nikki there, but he chose to remain in Central America and keep his vocation.

Robin returned to British Columbia, where she sought

counseling with an ex-priest on her relationship with Nikki's father, who had an intense vocation to protect the survival of his people and his country, even though the Catholic Church had essentially turned its back on his cause. The ex-priest was John, who cautioned her not to expect her priest to abandon his vows, so Robin raised her precocious young daughter alone, reengaged in the environmental movement, and finished her Ph.D. on Mayan education and the Mayan worldview.

After having heart surgery, Robin announced that it was time to heal, so she was going to look for someone that she could love again and provide a father to her daughter. She called me up shortly afterward and said that she had by chance met the same ex-priest who had once counseled her, and he had asked her out for coffee. What did I think? I urged her to go, as here was someone with the spiritual and activist grounding to match her own. As John reveals in his story, only an ex-radical theologian could have provided the insight into Robin's question and understand her long struggle.

When they met for the second time, John was a widow. He didn't just embrace Robin and Nikki into his life, he took in their whole community—and vice versa. I was one of the lucky ones to be swept into that constellation. One of John's inspirations, the quantum physicist David Bohm, says that an acorn is like a portal through which energy and matter pass to create the oak tree. Together, John and Robin created a portal through which all of our energy could pass to create an oak tree of support for this battered world. The portal is still there for you too, as John's reader.

Soon after the publication of the first edition of this book, when John contracted an incurable disease, he decided to be among the first British Columbians to elect for Medical Assistance in Dying (MAiD). The week before the date he elected to die on, his room at the hospice was filled with family and friends holding deep conversations about everything under the sun, including living and dying well. As John said, it was like an old-fashioned Irish wake, except that he was still alive. Each of us visitors had a chance to share our gratitude with him before he died. He also welcomed in a reporter from his hometown of New York City to follow his process. This was his final legacy: demonstrating how to die without fear in this grand, interconnected cosmos.

Acknowledgments

I have discovered that no book is simply the work of the author. It is the result of a collaboration between the author and a community in which love and goodwill come together to guide, enlighten, and improve the final product.

In the case of this book, the principal guides have been my wife, Robin June Hood, and my daughter Nikki, who both consistently urged me to reach deeper and to reveal more of the inner world that makes the fabric of my story. Robin read and reread versions from first to last, and called her good friend Briony Penn, the well-known Canadian writer, artist, educator, and environmentalist, for her valuable opinions and advice. Lynette Jackson also provided invaluable suggestions for a more polished manuscript.

I owe a great deal to the editor and writer Sylvia Taylor, who persuaded me to rethink my original concept for this book, and to turn it into a memoir. "Tell your story," she advised me. The conversations I had with Sylvia and Julie Salisbury, my publisher at Influence Publishing, Inc., took place at a crucial juncture and put me on a path to a richer narrative. To them, I cannot be more grateful. Julie's enthusiasm and faith in this project has been an inspiration from our first meeting.

My group of fellow authors, all of whom were meeting with Julie for the year during which I wrote the book, were a constant inspiration and support. Their encouragement and advice proved invaluable as I struggled to bring this project to completion.

I am grateful to Paul Bramadat, director of the Centre for the Study of Religion and Society at the University of Victoria, who provided a fellowship for me to work at the center. Having several months to concentrate on writing was a luxury, and to do so in the company of dedicated scholars was a treat for my spirit.

Walter Hood read the entire manuscript and was a steady support throughout, I am grateful to have him and Lorna Hood as my champions.

Thank you to friends like Cliff Stainsby, coworkers like Diane Wood, and teachers like Gerry Fewster, who have been a nurturing strength.

For the many other people I have not named but who supported me in this project, I am deeply thankful.

Over the years, scholars have guided me through their books and workshops. Chief among them are Briane Swimme, Thomas Berry, Peter Russell, and Joseph Campbell. These mentors played a profound role in shaping my spiritual quest.

CPSIA information can be obtained
at www.ICGtesting.com
Printed in the USA
JSHW012015261020
9118JS00002B/4